Playing out

TRAX
NIKE

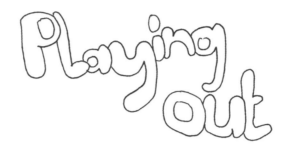

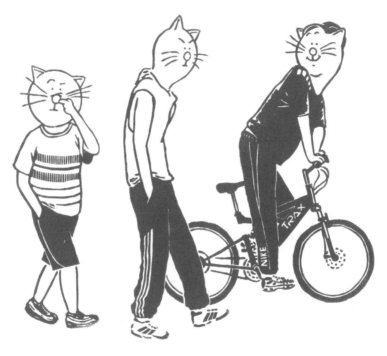

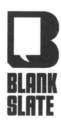

BLANK SLATE

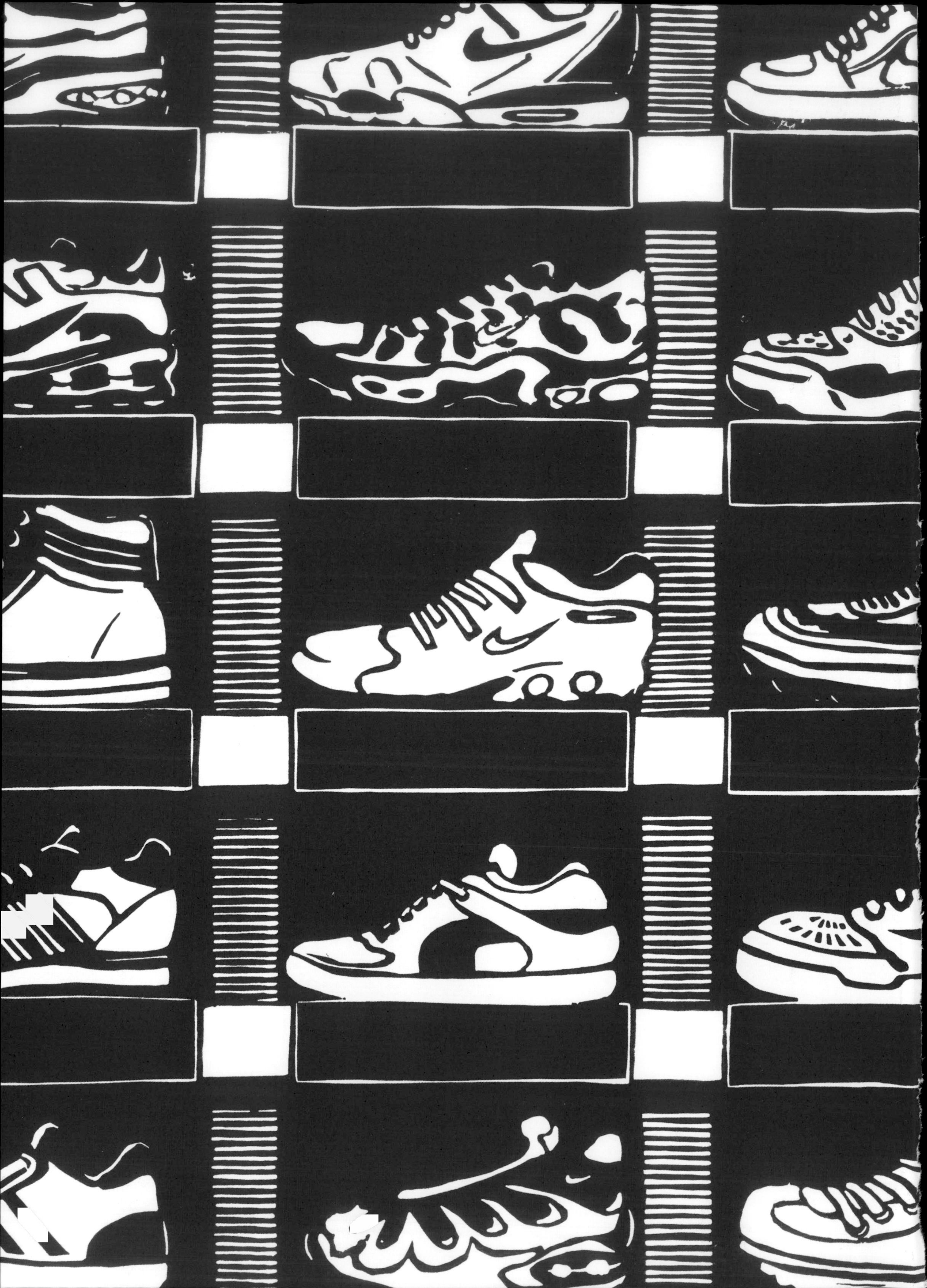

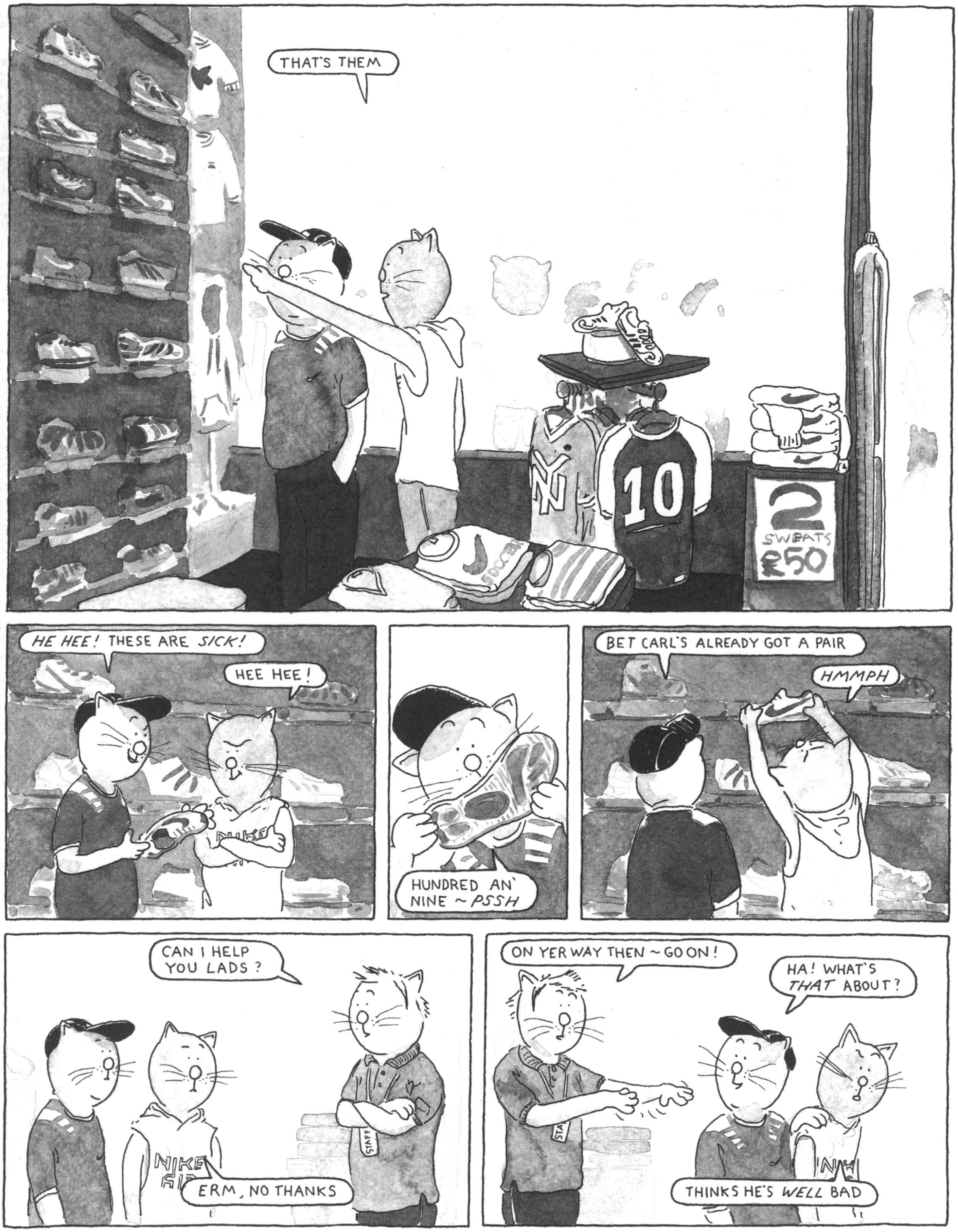
THAT'S THEM
10
2 SWEATS £50
HE HEE! THESE ARE *SICK*!
HEE HEE!
HUNDRED AN' NINE ~ *PSSH*
BET CARL'S ALREADY GOT A PAIR
HMMPH
CAN I HELP YOU LADS?
ERM, NO THANKS
ON YER WAY THEN ~ GO ON!
HA! WHAT'S *THAT* ABOUT?
THINKS HE'S *WELL* BAD

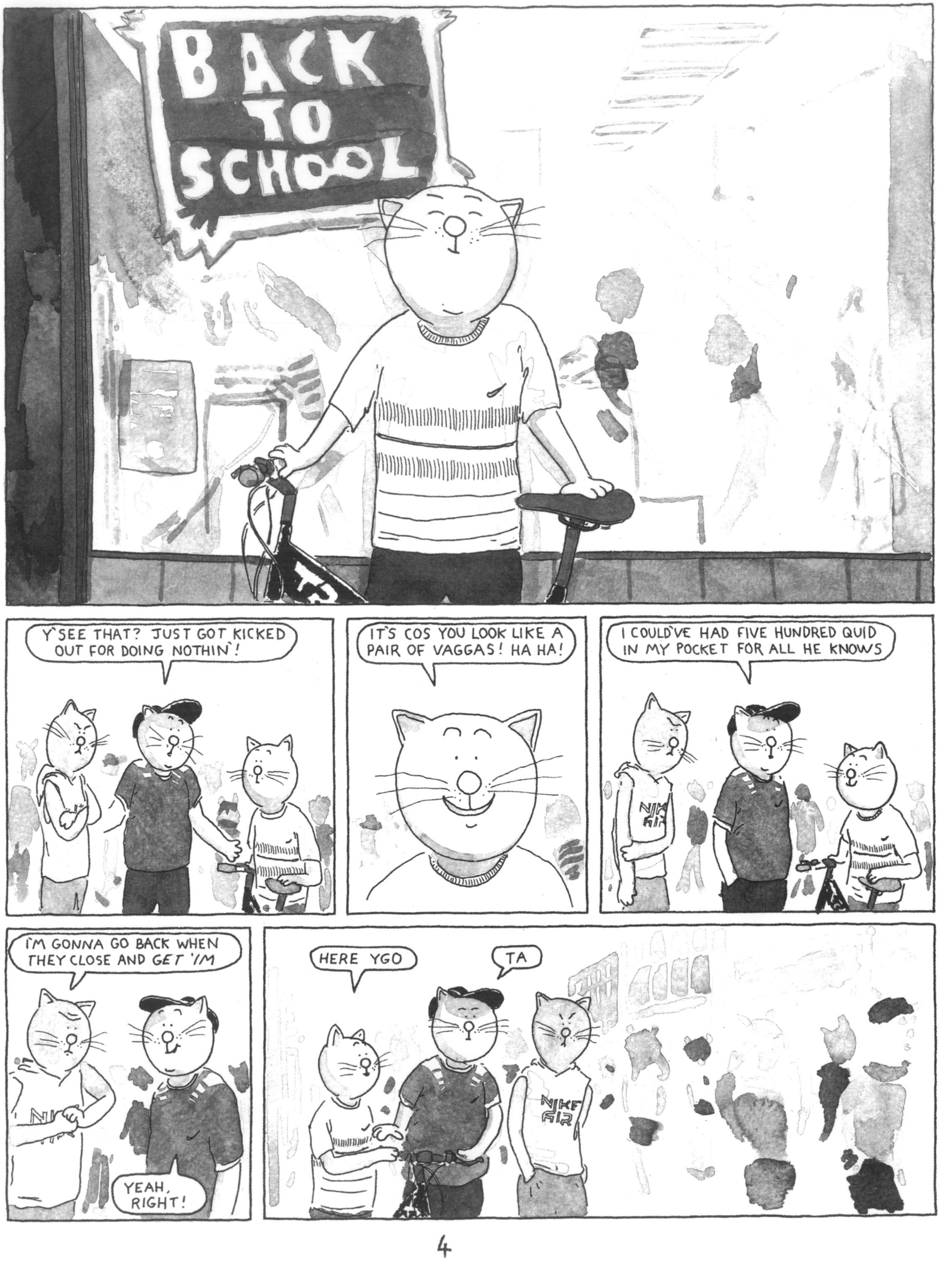
BACK TO SCHOOL
Y`SEE THAT? JUST GOT KICKED OUT FOR DOING NOTHIN`!
IT`S COS YOU LOOK LIKE A PAIR OF VAGGAS! HA HA!
I COULD`VE HAD FIVE HUNDRED QUID IN MY POCKET FOR ALL HE KNOWS
I`M GONNA GO BACK WHEN THEY CLOSE AND GET 'IM
YEAH, RIGHT!
HERE YGO
TA

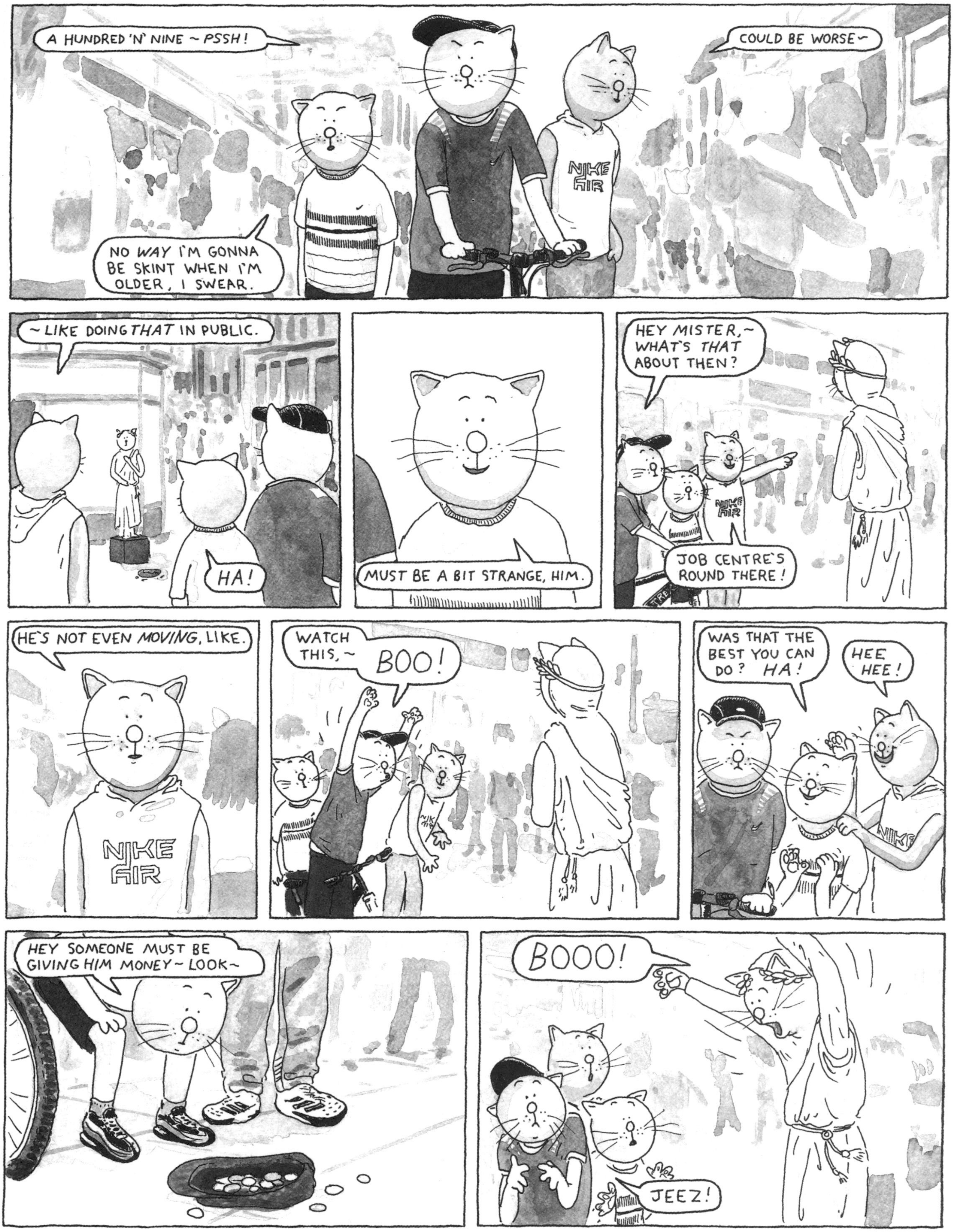
A HUNDRED 'N' NINE ~ PSSH!
COULD BE WORSE~
NO WAY I'M GONNA BE SKINT WHEN I'M OLDER, I SWEAR.
NIKE AIR
~ LIKE DOING THAT IN PUBLIC.
HA!
MUST BE A BIT STRANGE, HIM.
HEY MISTER,~ WHAT'S THAT ABOUT THEN?
JOB CENTRE'S ROUND THERE!
HE'S NOT EVEN MOVING, LIKE.
NIKE AIR
WATCH THIS,~
BOO!
WAS THAT THE BEST YOU CAN DO? HA!
HEE HEE!
HEY SOMEONE MUST BE GIVING HIM MONEY ~ LOOK~
BOOO!
JEEZ!

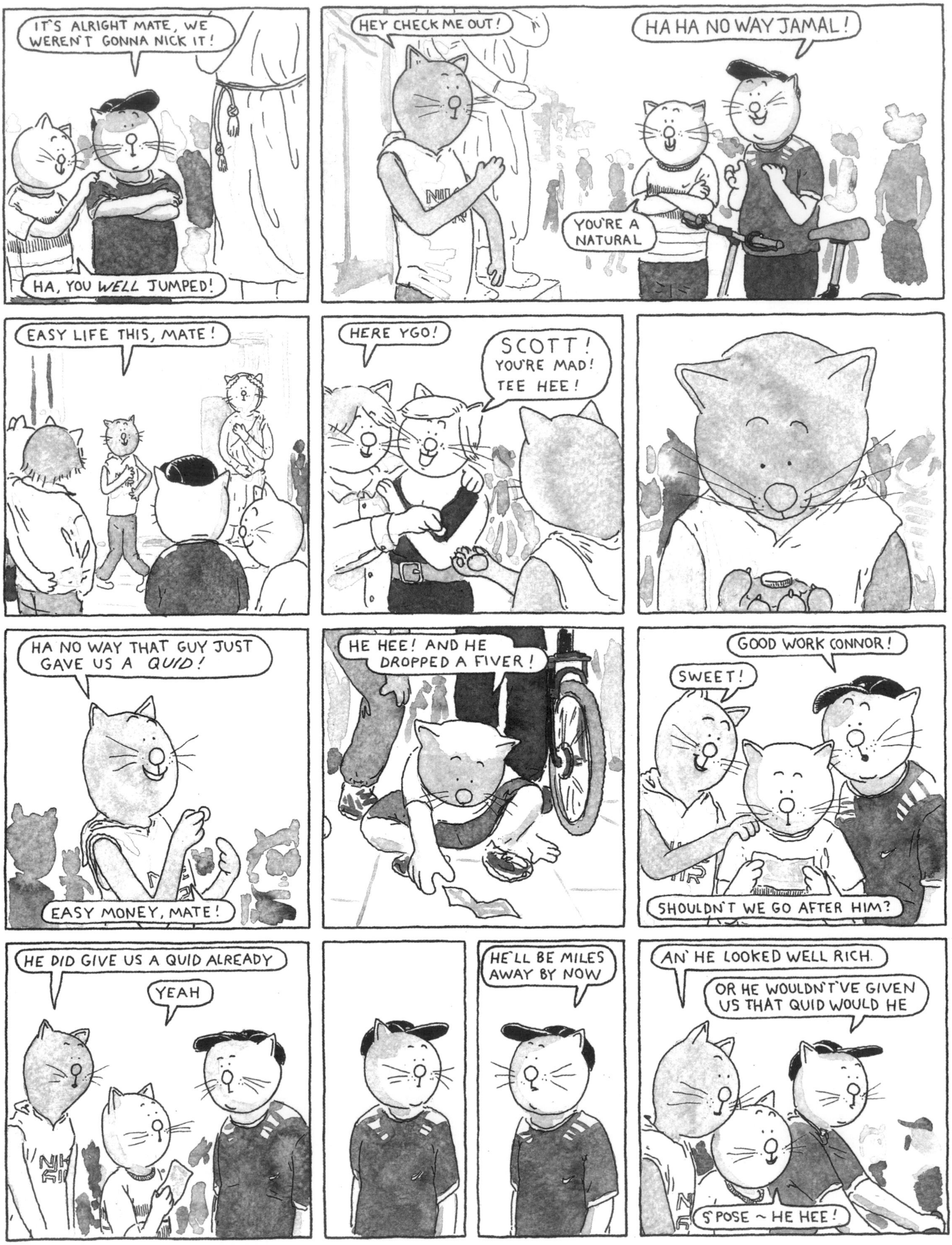
IT'S ALRIGHT MATE, WE WEREN'T GONNA NICK IT!
HA, YOU WELL JUMPED!
HEY CHECK ME OUT!
HA HA NO WAY JAMAL!
YOU'RE A NATURAL
EASY LIFE THIS, MATE!
HERE YGO!
SCOTT! YOU'RE MAD! TEE HEE!
HA NO WAY THAT GUY JUST GAVE US A QUID!
EASY MONEY, MATE!
HE HEE! AND HE DROPPED A FIVER!
GOOD WORK CONNOR!
SWEET!
SHOULDN'T WE GO AFTER HIM?
HE DID GIVE US A QUID ALREADY
YEAH
HE'LL BE MILES AWAY BY NOW
AN' HE LOOKED WELL RICH.
OR HE WOULDN'T'VE GIVEN US THAT QUID WOULD HE
S'POSE ~ HE HEE!

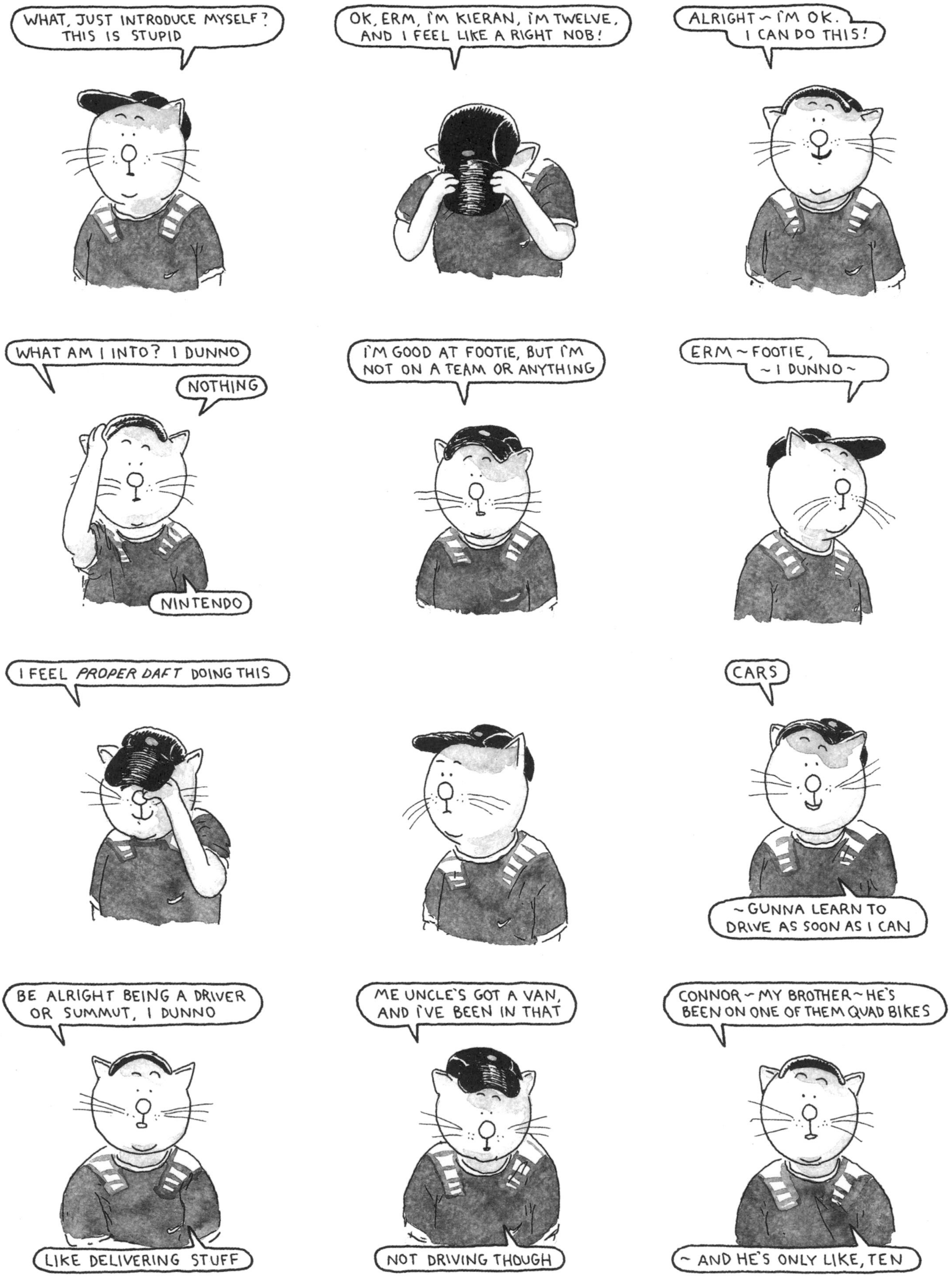
WHAT, JUST INTRODUCE MYSELF? THIS IS STUPID
OK, ERM, I'M KIERAN, I'M TWELVE, AND I FEEL LIKE A RIGHT NOB!
ALRIGHT ~ I'M OK. I CAN DO THIS!
WHAT AM I INTO? I DUNNO
NOTHING
NINTENDO
I'M GOOD AT FOOTIE, BUT I'M NOT ON A TEAM OR ANYTHING
ERM ~ FOOTIE, ~ I DUNNO ~
I FEEL *PROPER DAFT* DOING THIS
CARS
~ GUNNA LEARN TO DRIVE AS SOON AS I CAN
BE ALRIGHT BEING A DRIVER OR SUMMUT, I DUNNO
LIKE DELIVERING STUFF
ME UNCLE'S GOT A VAN, AND I'VE BEEN IN THAT
NOT DRIVING THOUGH
CONNOR ~ MY BROTHER ~ HE'S BEEN ON ONE OF THEM QUAD BIKES
~ AND HE'S ONLY LIKE, TEN

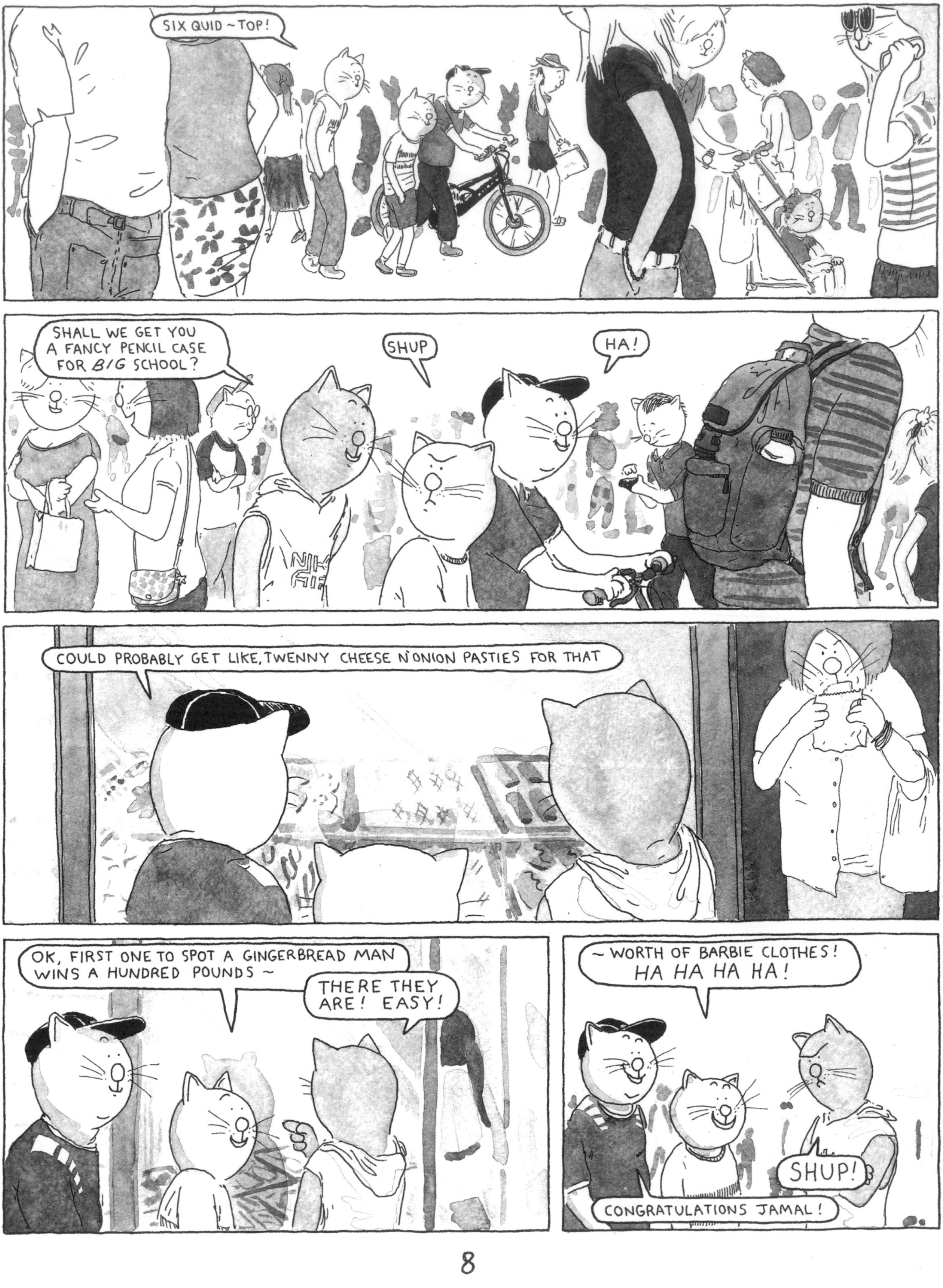
SIX QUID ~ TOP!
SHALL WE GET YOU A FANCY PENCIL CASE FOR BIG SCHOOL?
SHUP
HA!
COULD PROBABLY GET LIKE, TWENNY CHEESE N'ONION PASTIES FOR THAT
OK, FIRST ONE TO SPOT A GINGERBREAD MAN WINS A HUNDRED POUNDS ~
THERE THEY ARE! EASY!
~ WORTH OF BARBIE CLOTHES! HA HA HA HA!
SHUP!
CONGRATULATIONS JAMAL!

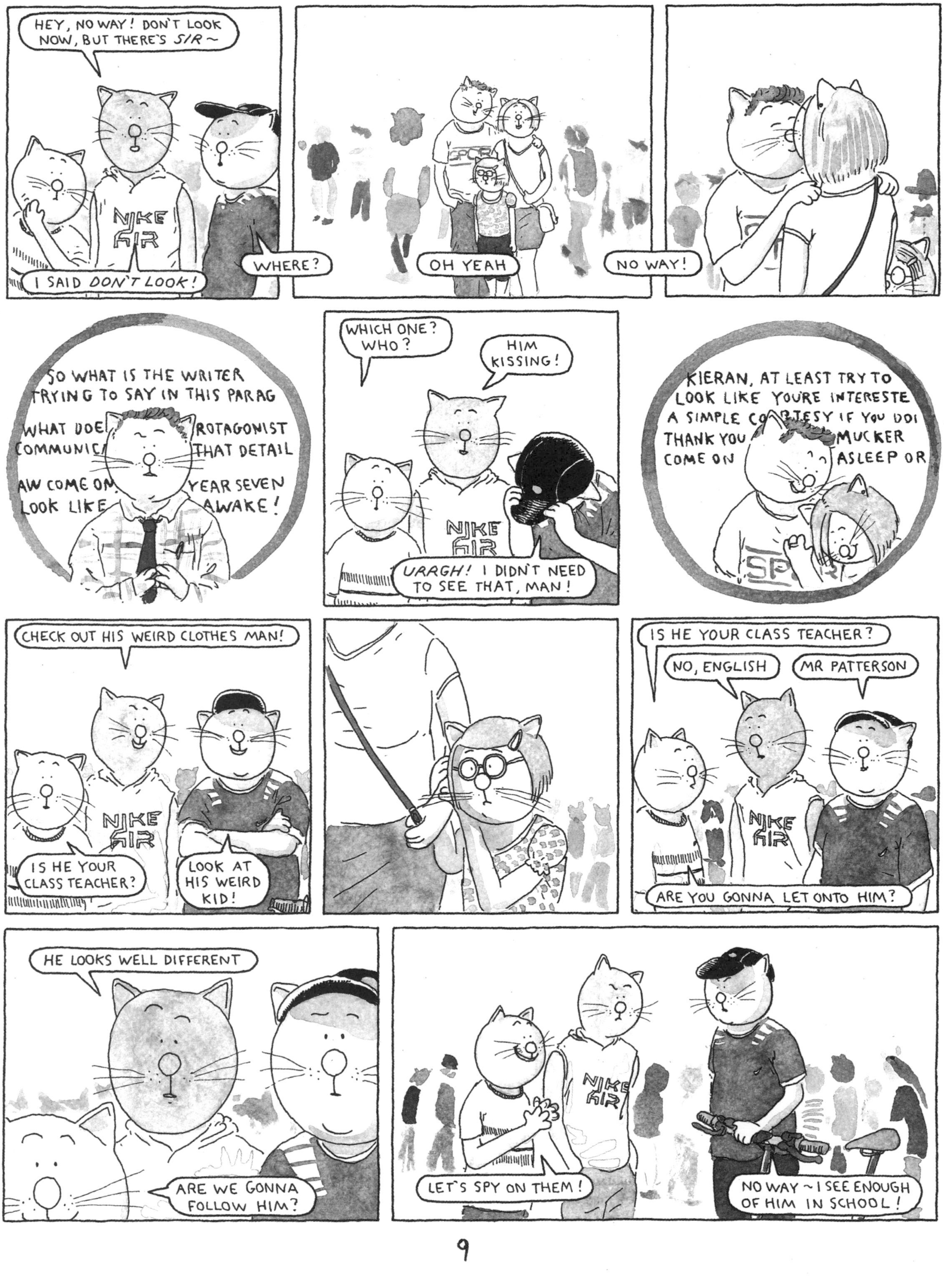
HEY, NO WAY! DON'T LOOK NOW, BUT THERE'S SIR ~
I SAID DON'T LOOK!
WHERE?
OH YEAH
NO WAY!
SO WHAT IS THE WRITER TRYING TO SAY IN THIS PARAG
WHAT DOE
ROTAGONIST
COMMUNIC
THAT DETAIL
AW COME ON
YEAR SEVEN
LOOK LIKE
AWAKE!
WHICH ONE? WHO?
HIM KISSING!
URAGH! I DIDN'T NEED TO SEE THAT, MAN!
KIERAN, AT LEAST TRY TO LOOK LIKE YOU'RE INTERESTE
A SIMPLE CO RTESY IF YOU DOI
THANK YOU
MUCKER
COME ON
ASLEEP OR
CHECK OUT HIS WEIRD CLOTHES MAN!
IS HE YOUR CLASS TEACHER?
LOOK AT HIS WEIRD KID!
IS HE YOUR CLASS TEACHER?
NO, ENGLISH
MR PATTERSON
ARE YOU GONNA LET ONTO HIM?
HE LOOKS WELL DIFFERENT
ARE WE GONNA FOLLOW HIM?
LET'S SPY ON THEM!
NO WAY ~ I SEE ENOUGH OF HIM IN SCHOOL!

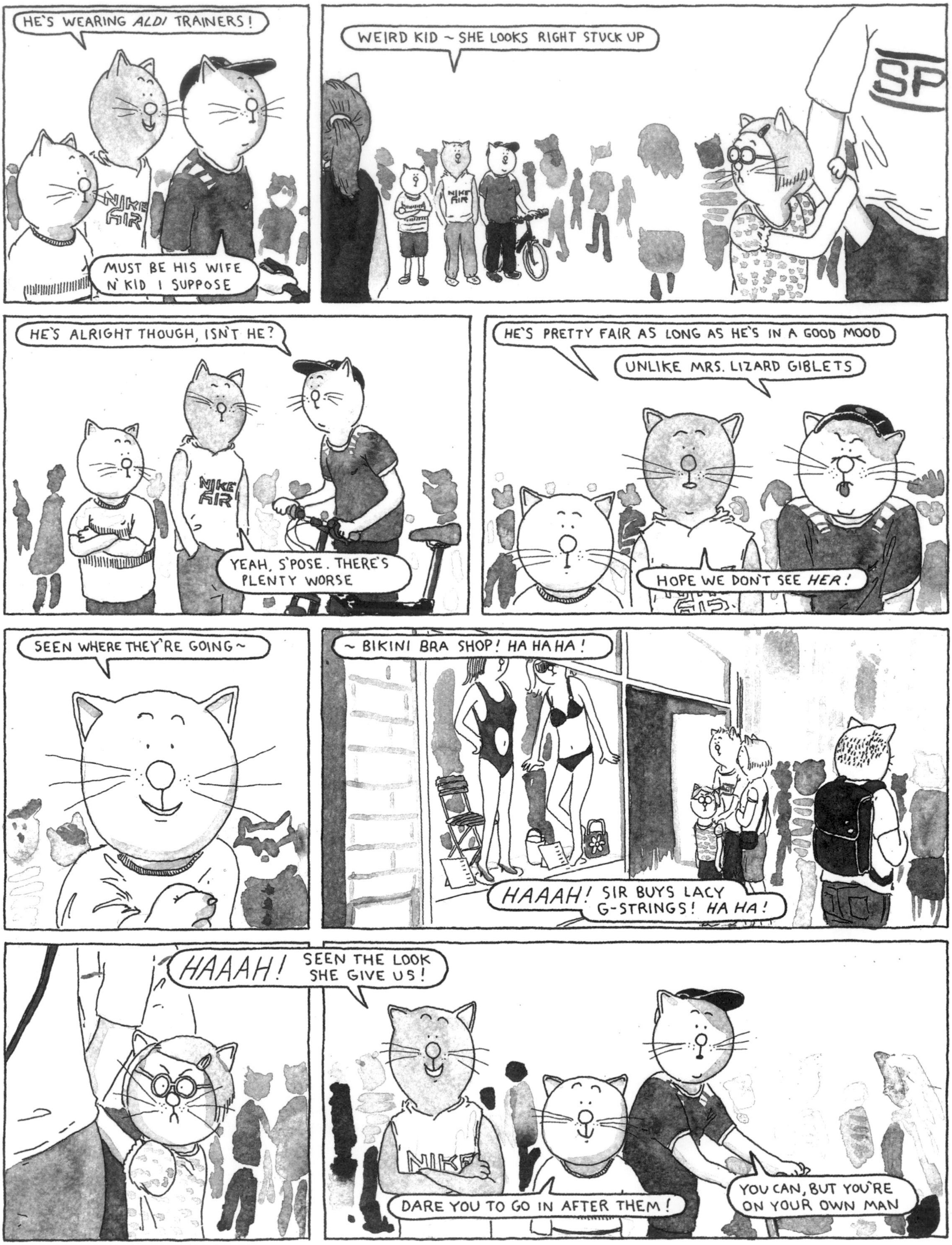
HE'S WEARING ALDI TRAINERS!
MUST BE HIS WIFE N' KID I SUPPOSE
WEIRD KID ~ SHE LOOKS RIGHT STUCK UP
SP
NIKE AIR
HE'S ALRIGHT THOUGH, ISN'T HE?
YEAH, S'POSE. THERE'S PLENTY WORSE
HE'S PRETTY FAIR AS LONG AS HE'S IN A GOOD MOOD
UNLIKE MRS. LIZARD GIBLETS
HOPE WE DON'T SEE HER!
SEEN WHERE THEY'RE GOING ~
~ BIKINI BRA SHOP! HA HA HA!
HAAAH! SIR BUYS LACY G-STRINGS! HA HA!
HAAAH! SEEN THE LOOK SHE GIVE US!
DARE YOU TO GO IN AFTER THEM!
YOU CAN, BUT YOU'RE ON YOUR OWN MAN

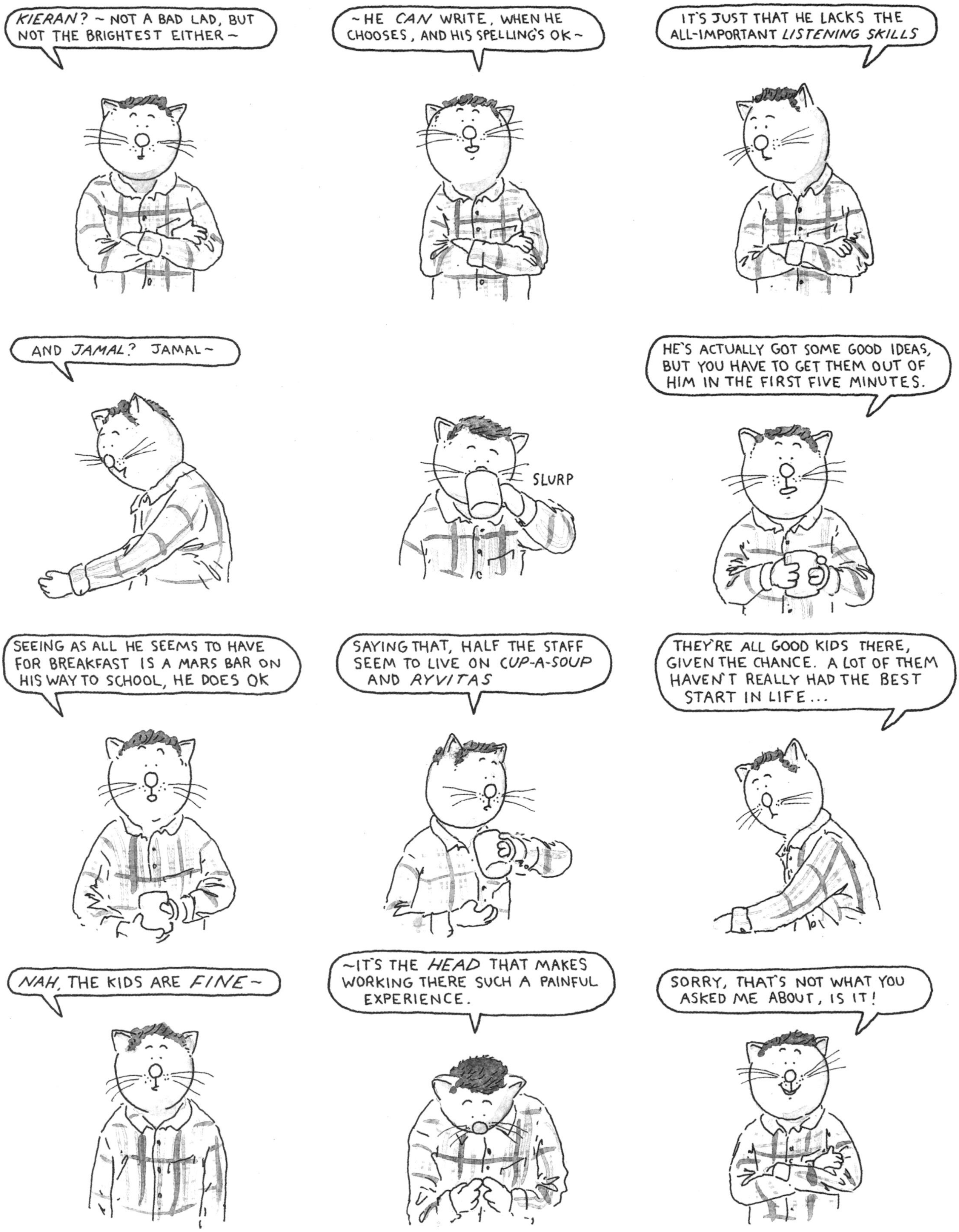
KIERAN? ~ NOT A BAD LAD, BUT NOT THE BRIGHTEST EITHER ~
~ HE CAN WRITE, WHEN HE CHOOSES, AND HIS SPELLING'S OK ~
IT'S JUST THAT HE LACKS THE ALL-IMPORTANT LISTENING SKILLS
AND JAMAL? JAMAL ~
SLURP
HE'S ACTUALLY GOT SOME GOOD IDEAS, BUT YOU HAVE TO GET THEM OUT OF HIM IN THE FIRST FIVE MINUTES.
SEEING AS ALL HE SEEMS TO HAVE FOR BREAKFAST IS A MARS BAR ON HIS WAY TO SCHOOL, HE DOES OK
SAYING THAT, HALF THE STAFF SEEM TO LIVE ON CUP-A-SOUP AND RYVITAS
THEY'RE ALL GOOD KIDS THERE, GIVEN THE CHANCE. A LOT OF THEM HAVEN'T REALLY HAD THE BEST START IN LIFE...
NAH, THE KIDS ARE FINE ~
~ IT'S THE HEAD THAT MAKES WORKING THERE SUCH A PAINFUL EXPERIENCE.
SORRY, THAT'S NOT WHAT YOU ASKED ME ABOUT, IS IT!

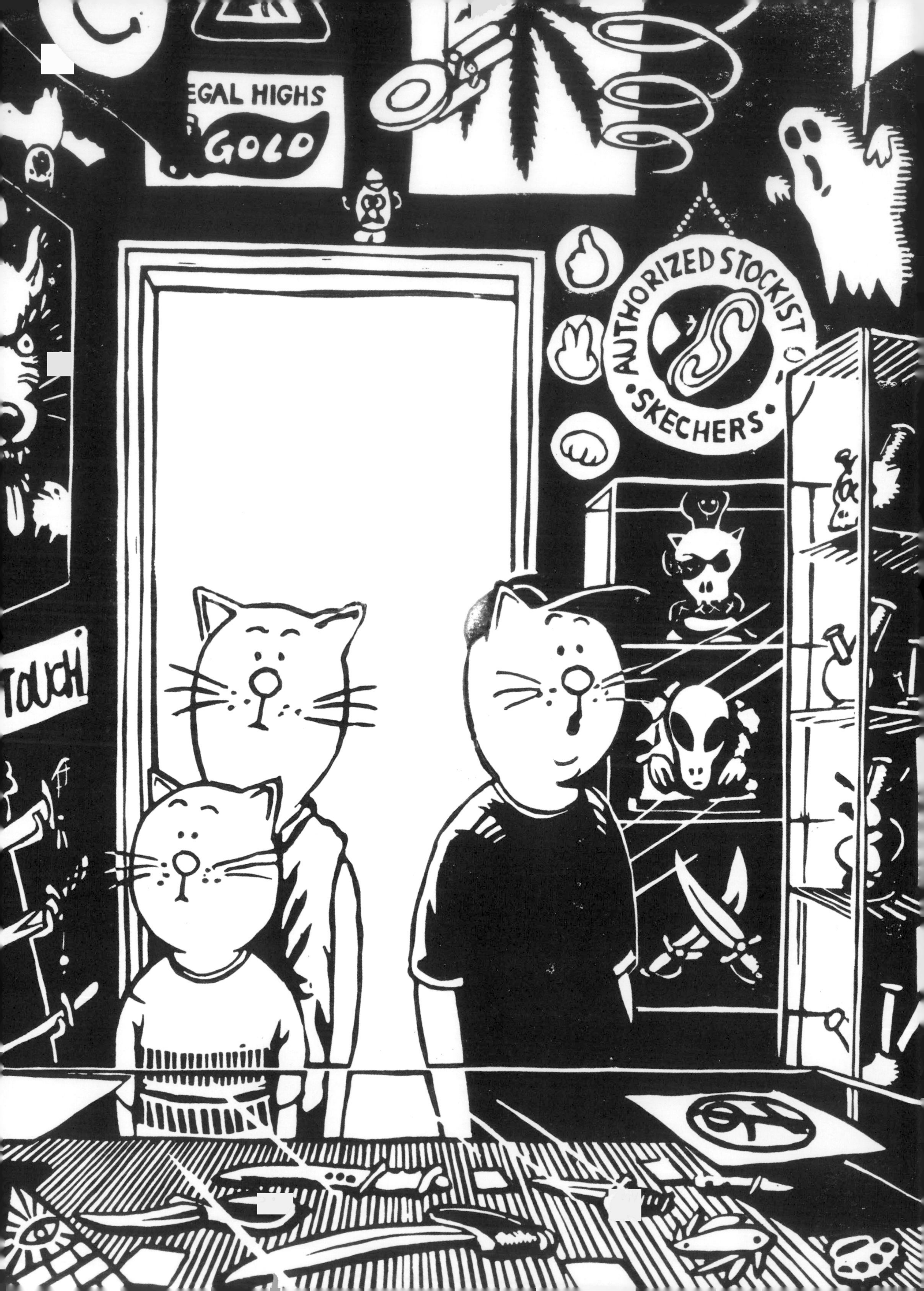
EGAL HIGHS
GOLD
AUTHORIZED STOCKIST
SKECHERS
TOUCH

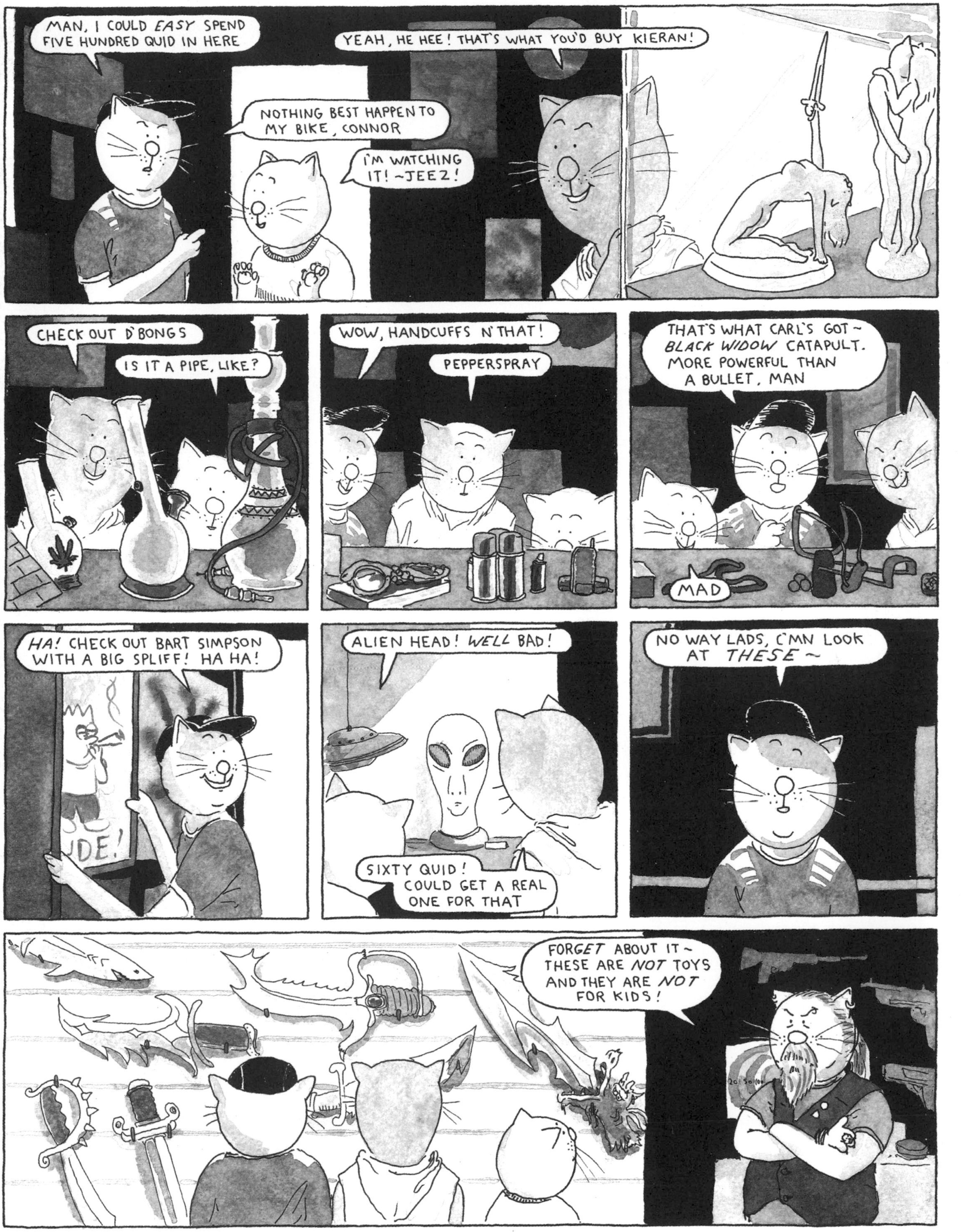
MAN, I COULD EASY SPEND FIVE HUNDRED QUID IN HERE
NOTHING BEST HAPPEN TO MY BIKE, CONNOR
I'M WATCHING IT! ~JEEZ!
YEAH, HE HEE! THAT'S WHAT YOU'D BUY KIERAN!
CHECK OUT D'BONGS
IS IT A PIPE, LIKE?
WOW, HANDCUFFS N'THAT!
PEPPERSPRAY
THAT'S WHAT CARL'S GOT ~ BLACK WIDOW CATAPULT. MORE POWERFUL THAN A BULLET, MAN
MAD
HA! CHECK OUT BART SIMPSON WITH A BIG SPLIFF! HA HA!
UDE!
ALIEN HEAD! WELL BAD!
SIXTY QUID! COULD GET A REAL ONE FOR THAT
NO WAY LADS, C'MN LOOK AT THESE ~
FORGET ABOUT IT ~ THESE ARE NOT TOYS AND THEY ARE NOT FOR KIDS!

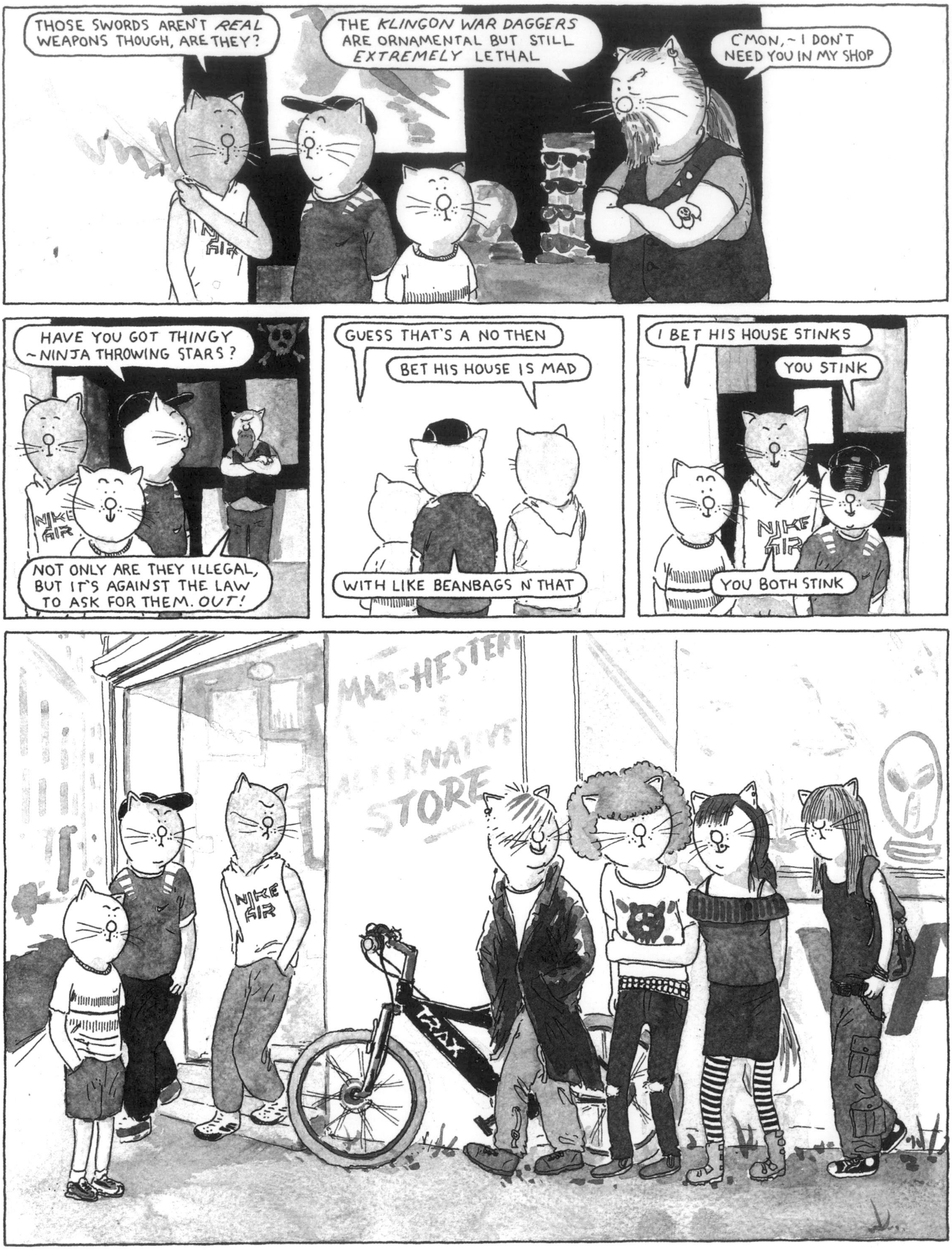
THOSE SWORDS AREN'T REAL WEAPONS THOUGH, ARE THEY?
THE KLINGON WAR DAGGERS ARE ORNAMENTAL BUT STILL EXTREMELY LETHAL
C'MON, ~ I DON'T NEED YOU IN MY SHOP
HAVE YOU GOT THINGY ~ NINJA THROWING STARS?
NOT ONLY ARE THEY ILLEGAL, BUT IT'S AGAINST THE LAW TO ASK FOR THEM. OUT!
GUESS THAT'S A NO THEN
BET HIS HOUSE IS MAD
WITH LIKE BEANBAGS N' THAT
I BET HIS HOUSE STINKS
YOU STINK
YOU BOTH STINK
MANCHESTER
ALTERNATIVE
STORE

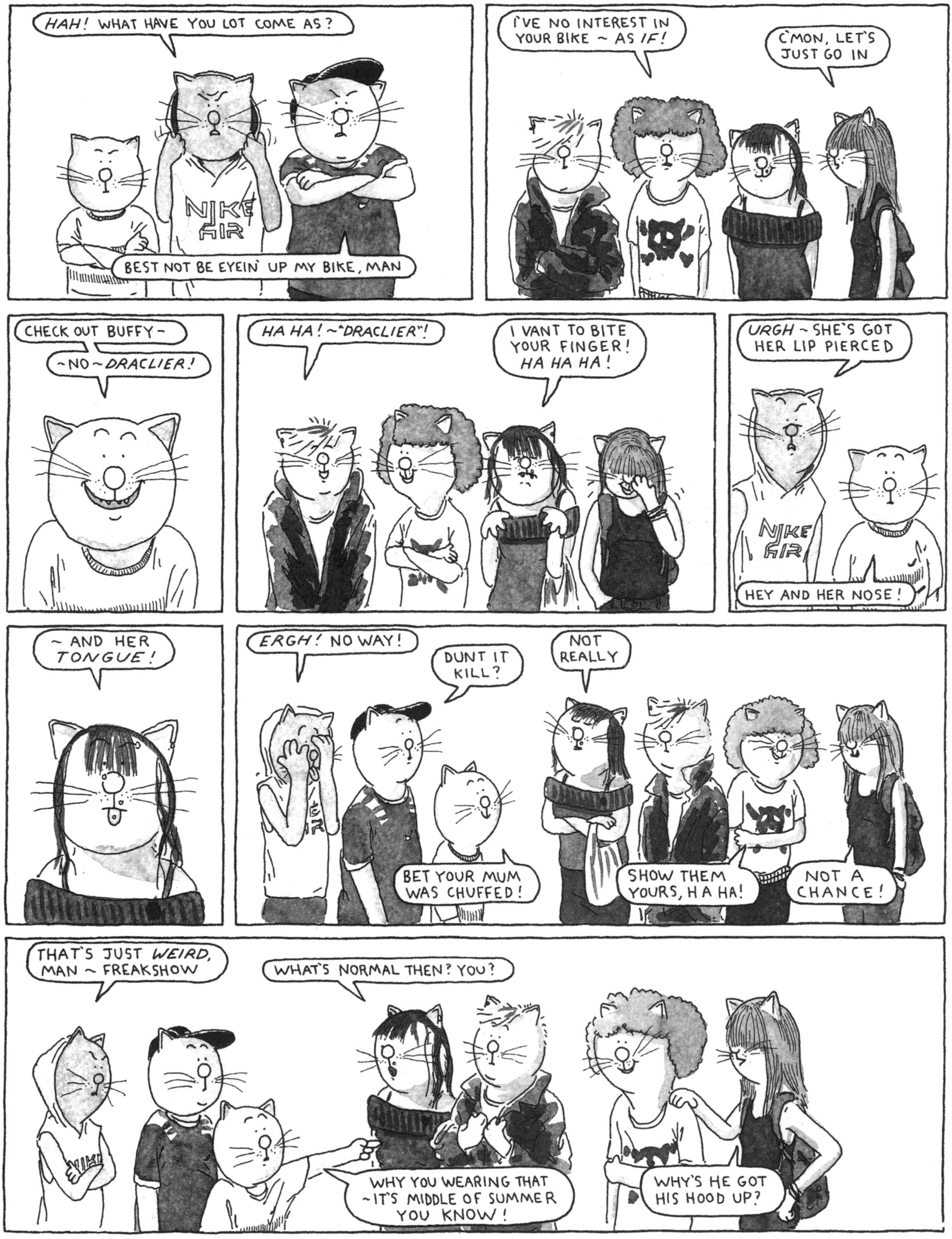

HAH! WHAT HAVE YOU LOT COME AS?
BEST NOT BE EYEIN' UP MY BIKE, MAN
I'VE NO INTEREST IN YOUR BIKE ~ AS IF!
C'MON, LET'S JUST GO IN
CHECK OUT BUFFY~
~NO~DRACLIER!
HA HA! ~"DRACLIER"!
I VANT TO BITE YOUR FINGER! HA HA HA!
URGH ~ SHE'S GOT HER LIP PIERCED
HEY AND HER NOSE!
~ AND HER TONGUE!
ERGH! NO WAY!
DUNT IT KILL?
NOT REALLY
BET YOUR MUM WAS CHUFFED!
SHOW THEM YOURS, HA HA!
NOT A CHANCE!
THAT'S JUST WEIRD, MAN ~ FREAKSHOW
WHAT'S NORMAL THEN? YOU?
WHY YOU WEARING THAT ~IT'S MIDDLE OF SUMMER YOU KNOW!
WHY'S HE GOT HIS HOOD UP?

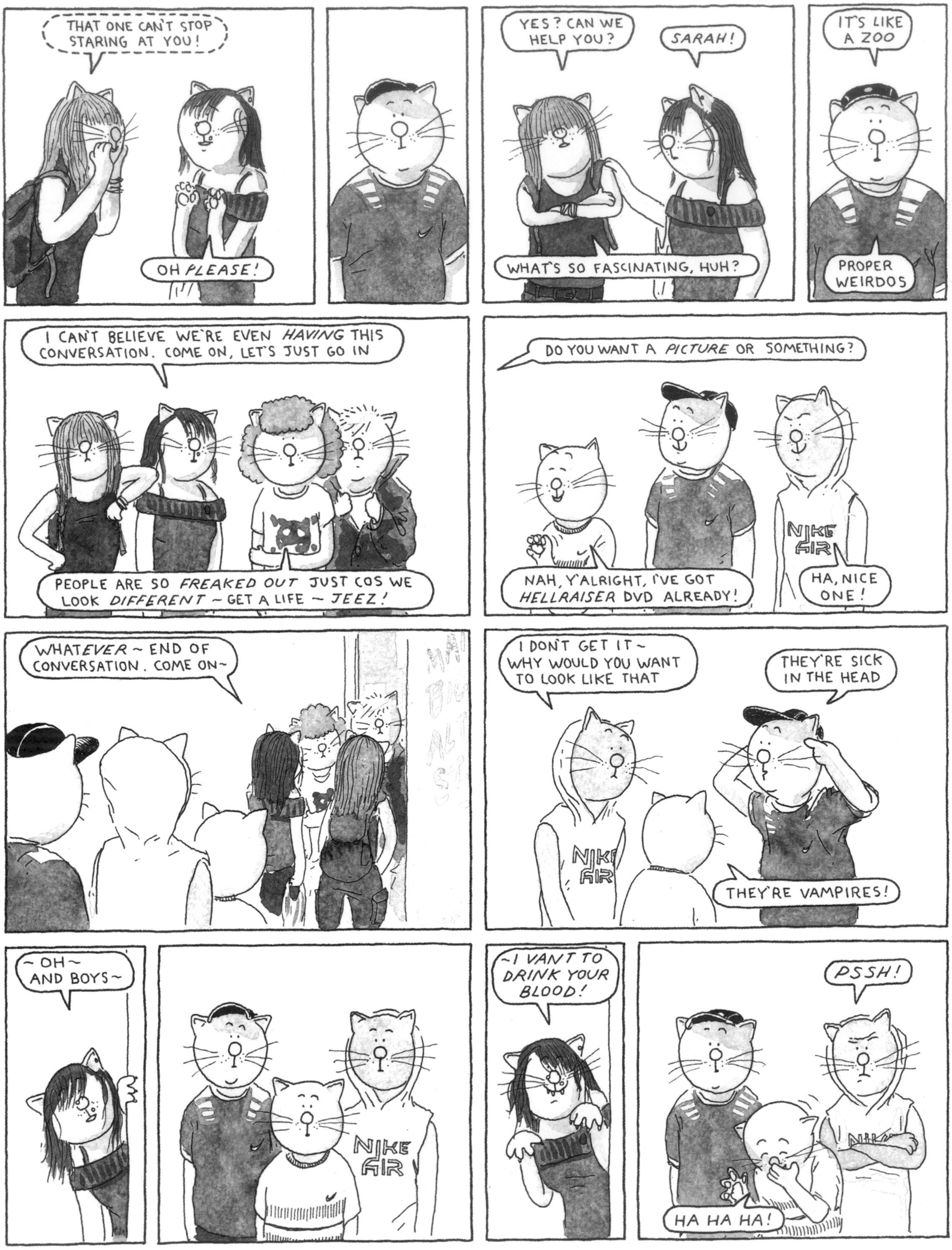
THAT ONE CAN'T STOP STARING AT YOU!
OH PLEASE!
YES? CAN WE HELP YOU?
SARAH!
WHAT'S SO FASCINATING, HUH?
IT'S LIKE A ZOO
PROPER WEIRDOS
I CAN'T BELIEVE WE'RE EVEN HAVING THIS CONVERSATION. COME ON, LET'S JUST GO IN
PEOPLE ARE SO FREAKED OUT JUST COS WE LOOK DIFFERENT ~ GET A LIFE ~ JEEZ!
DO YOU WANT A PICTURE OR SOMETHING?
NAH, Y'ALRIGHT, I'VE GOT HELLRAISER DVD ALREADY!
HA, NICE ONE!
WHATEVER ~ END OF CONVERSATION. COME ON~
I DON'T GET IT ~ WHY WOULD YOU WANT TO LOOK LIKE THAT
THEY'RE SICK IN THE HEAD
THEY'RE VAMPIRES!
~ OH ~ AND BOYS ~
~ I VANT TO DRINK YOUR BLOOD!
PSSH!
HA HA HA!

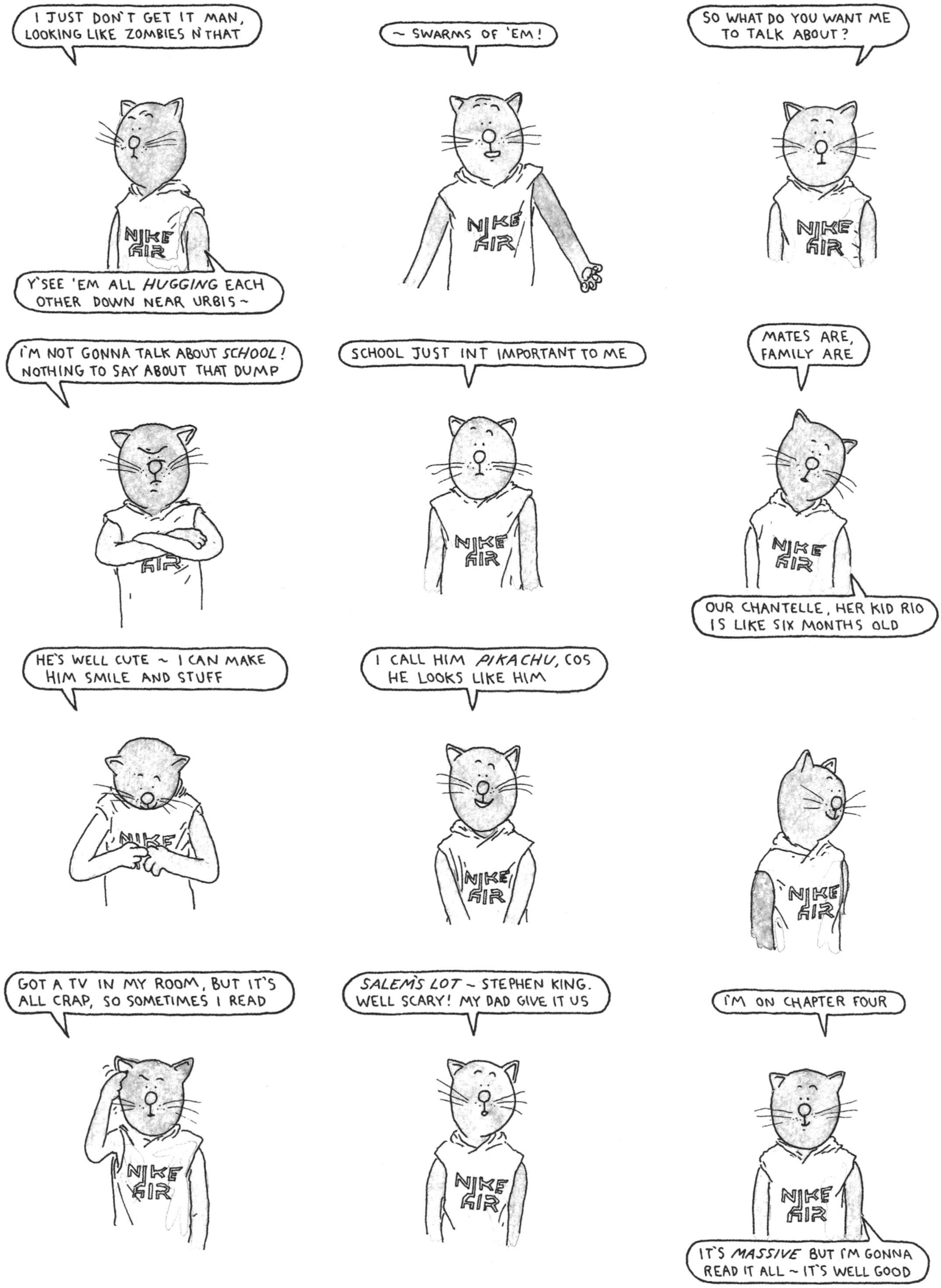
I JUST DON'T GET IT MAN, LOOKING LIKE ZOMBIES N'THAT
Y'SEE 'EM ALL *HUGGING* EACH OTHER DOWN NEAR URBIS ~
~ SWARMS OF 'EM!
SO WHAT DO YOU WANT ME TO TALK ABOUT?
I'M NOT GONNA TALK ABOUT *SCHOOL*! NOTHING TO SAY ABOUT THAT DUMP
SCHOOL JUST INT IMPORTANT TO ME
MATES ARE, FAMILY ARE
OUR CHANTELLE, HER KID RIO IS LIKE SIX MONTHS OLD
HE'S WELL CUTE ~ I CAN MAKE HIM SMILE AND STUFF
I CALL HIM *PIKACHU*, COS HE LOOKS LIKE HIM
GOT A TV IN MY ROOM, BUT IT'S ALL CRAP, SO SOMETIMES I READ
SALEM'S LOT ~ STEPHEN KING. WELL SCARY! MY DAD GIVE IT US
I'M ON CHAPTER FOUR
IT'S *MASSIVE* BUT I'M GONNA READ IT ALL ~ IT'S WELL GOOD

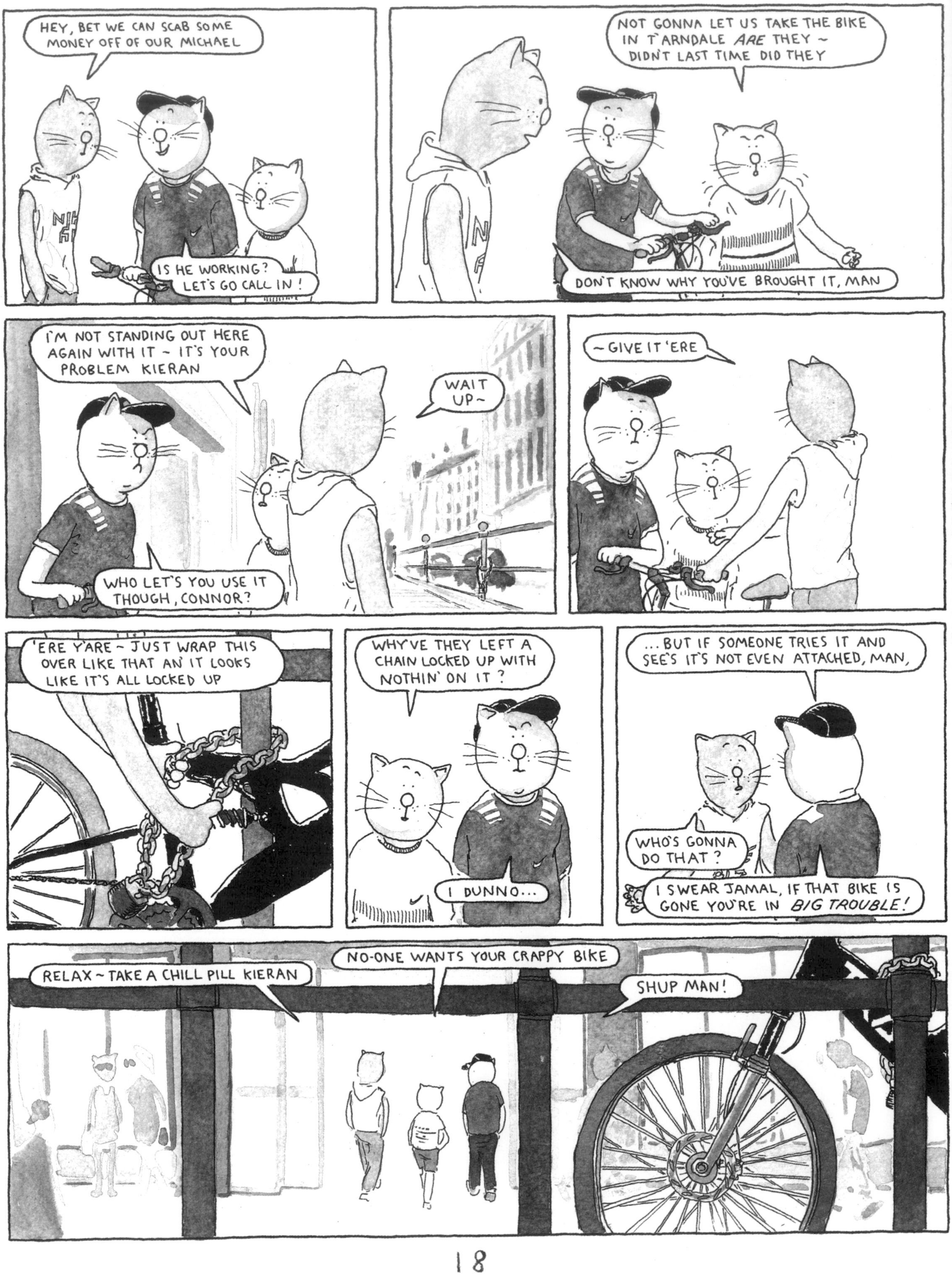
HEY, BET WE CAN SCAB SOME MONEY OFF OF OUR MICHAEL
IS HE WORKING? LET'S GO CALL IN!
NOT GONNA LET US TAKE THE BIKE IN T'ARNDALE *ARE* THEY ~ DIDN'T LAST TIME DID THEY
DON'T KNOW WHY YOU'VE BROUGHT IT, MAN
I'M NOT STANDING OUT HERE AGAIN WITH IT ~ IT'S YOUR PROBLEM KIERAN
WAIT UP~
WHO LET'S YOU USE IT THOUGH, CONNOR?
~ GIVE IT 'ERE
'ERE Y'ARE ~ JUST WRAP THIS OVER LIKE THAT AN' IT LOOKS LIKE IT'S ALL LOCKED UP
WHY'VE THEY LEFT A CHAIN LOCKED UP WITH NOTHIN' ON IT?
I DUNNO...
... BUT IF SOMEONE TRIES IT AND SEE'S IT'S NOT EVEN ATTACHED, MAN,
WHO'S GONNA DO THAT?
I SWEAR JAMAL, IF THAT BIKE IS GONE YOU'RE IN *BIG TROUBLE*!
RELAX ~ TAKE A CHILL PILL KIERAN
NO-ONE WANTS YOUR CRAPPY BIKE
SHUP MAN!

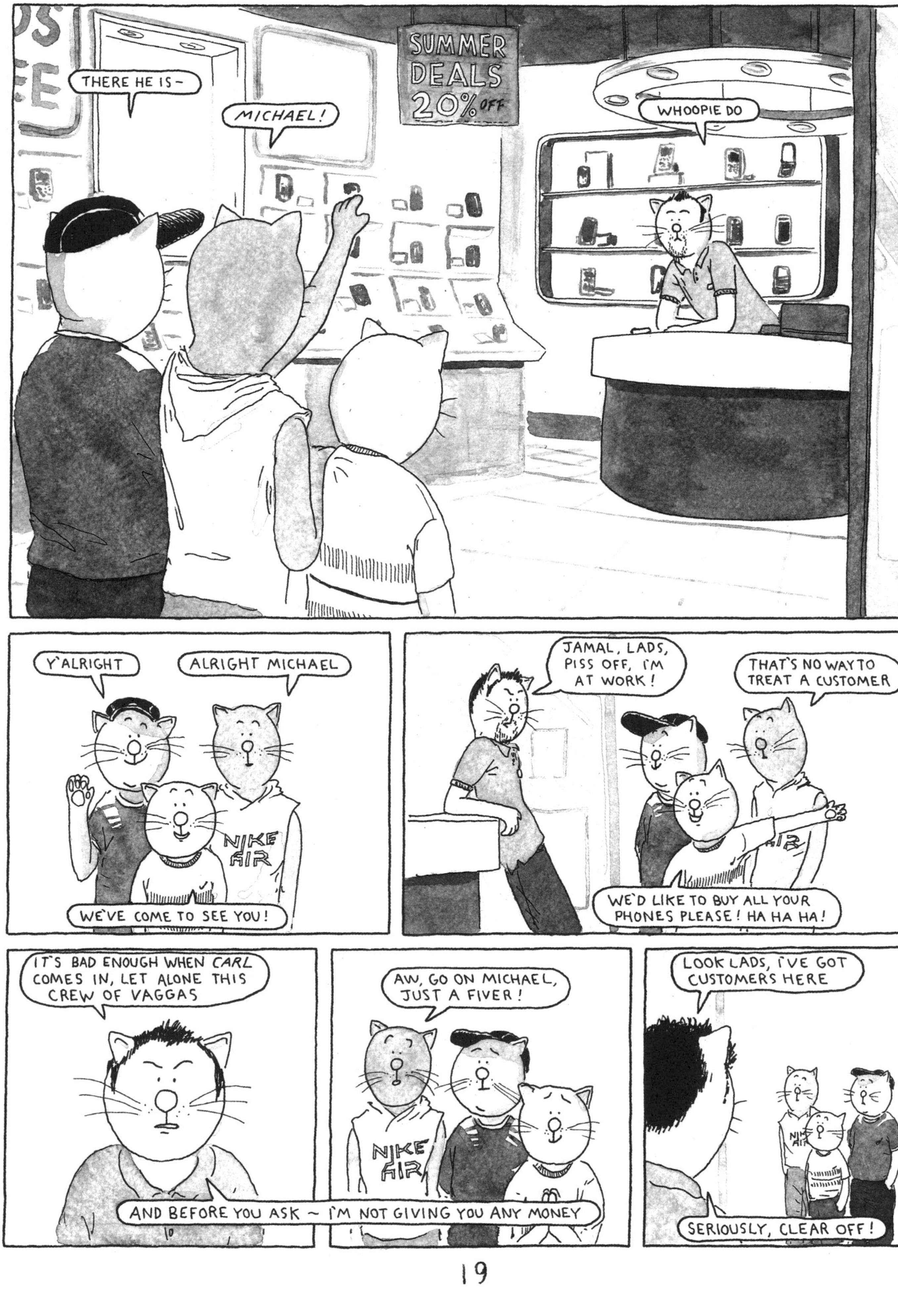

SUMMER DEALS 20% OFF
THERE HE IS -
MICHAEL!
WHOOPIE DO
Y'ALRIGHT
ALRIGHT MICHAEL
WE'VE COME TO SEE YOU!
NIKE AIR
JAMAL, LADS, PISS OFF, I'M AT WORK!
THAT'S NO WAY TO TREAT A CUSTOMER
WE'D LIKE TO BUY ALL YOUR PHONES PLEASE! HA HA HA!
IT'S BAD ENOUGH WHEN CARL COMES IN, LET ALONE THIS CREW OF VAGGAS
AW, GO ON MICHAEL, JUST A FIVER!
AND BEFORE YOU ASK ~ I'M NOT GIVING YOU ANY MONEY
LOOK LADS, I'VE GOT CUSTOMERS HERE
SERIOUSLY, CLEAR OFF!

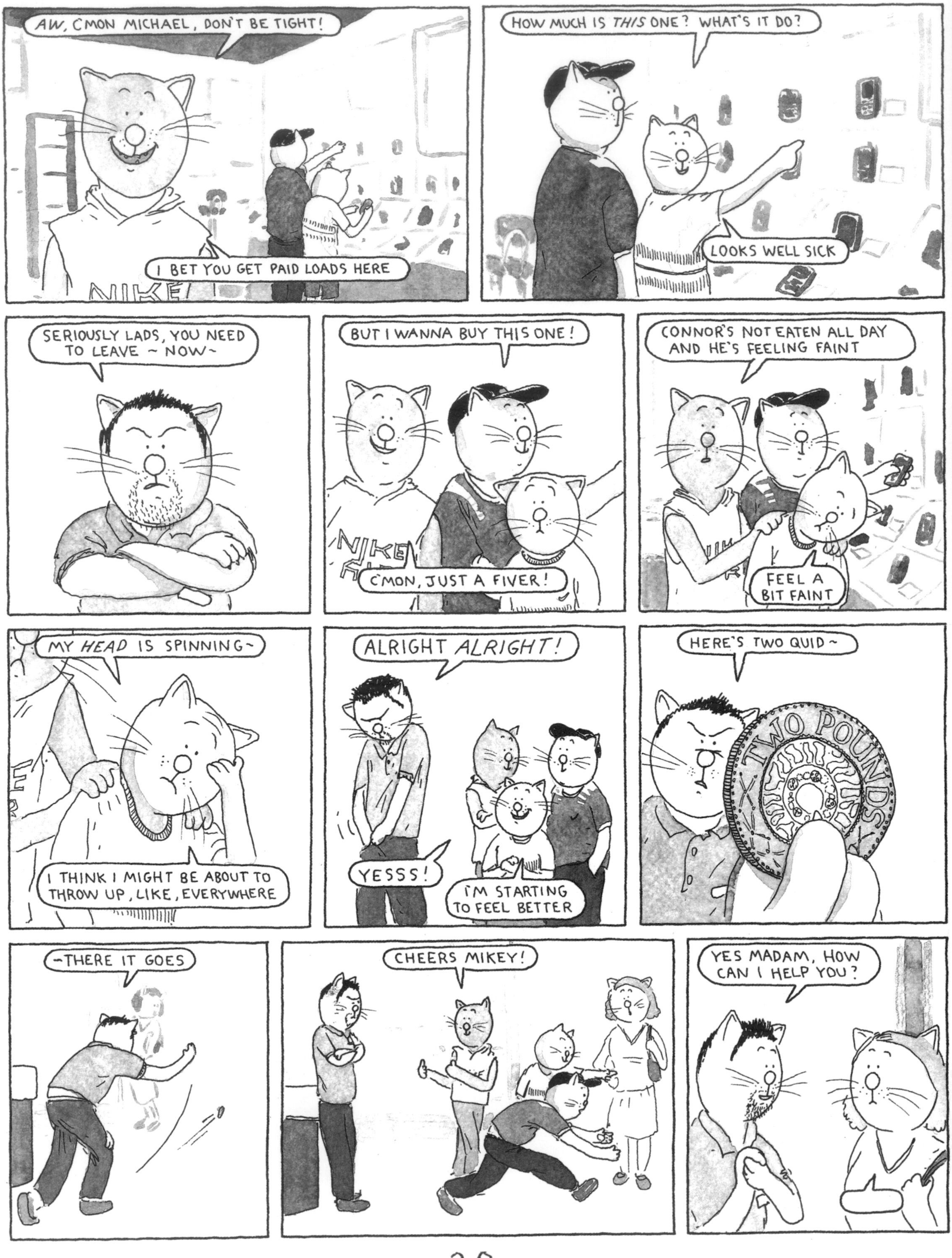
AW, C'MON MICHAEL, DON'T BE TIGHT!
I BET YOU GET PAID LOADS HERE
NIKE
HOW MUCH IS *THIS* ONE? WHAT'S IT DO?
LOOKS WELL SICK
SERIOUSLY LADS, YOU NEED TO LEAVE ~ NOW ~
BUT I WANNA BUY THIS ONE!
C'MON, JUST A FIVER!
CONNOR'S NOT EATEN ALL DAY AND HE'S FEELING FAINT
FEEL A BIT FAINT
MY *HEAD* IS SPINNING ~
I THINK I MIGHT BE ABOUT TO THROW UP, LIKE, EVERYWHERE
ALRIGHT *ALRIGHT*!
YESSS!
I'M STARTING TO FEEL BETTER
HERE'S TWO QUID ~
TWO POUNDS
~THERE IT GOES
CHEERS MIKEY!
YES MADAM, HOW CAN I HELP YOU?

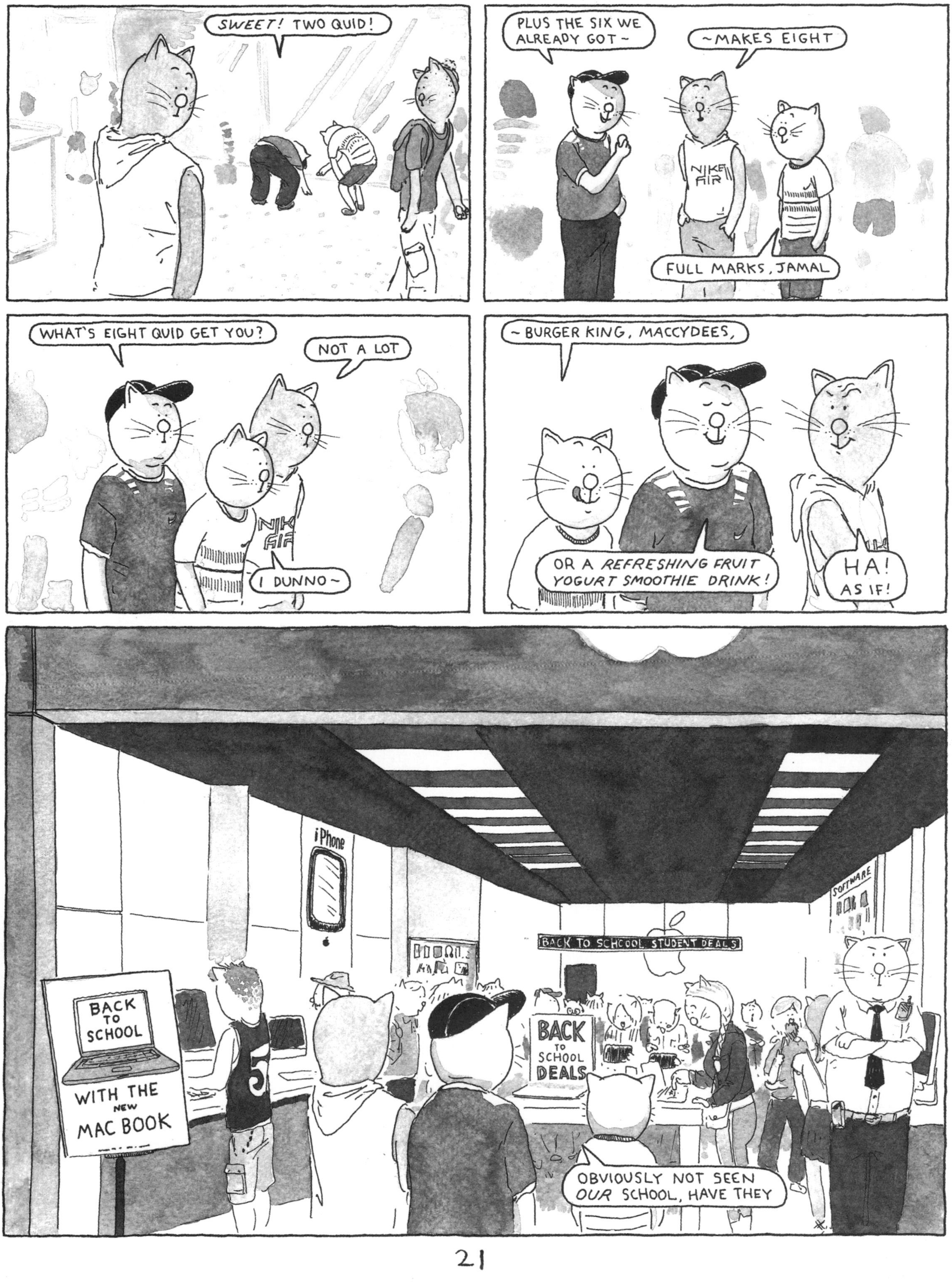
SWEET! TWO QUID!
PLUS THE SIX WE ALREADY GOT~
~MAKES EIGHT
NIKE AIR
FULL MARKS, JAMAL
WHAT'S EIGHT QUID GET YOU?
NOT A LOT
I DUNNO~
~BURGER KING, MACCYDEES,
OR A REFRESHING FRUIT YOGURT SMOOTHIE DRINK!
HA! AS IF!
iPhone
SOFTWARE
BACK TO SCHOOL STUDENT DEALS
BACK TO SCHOOL WITH THE NEW MAC BOOK
BACK TO SCHOOL DEALS
OBVIOUSLY NOT SEEN OUR SCHOOL, HAVE THEY

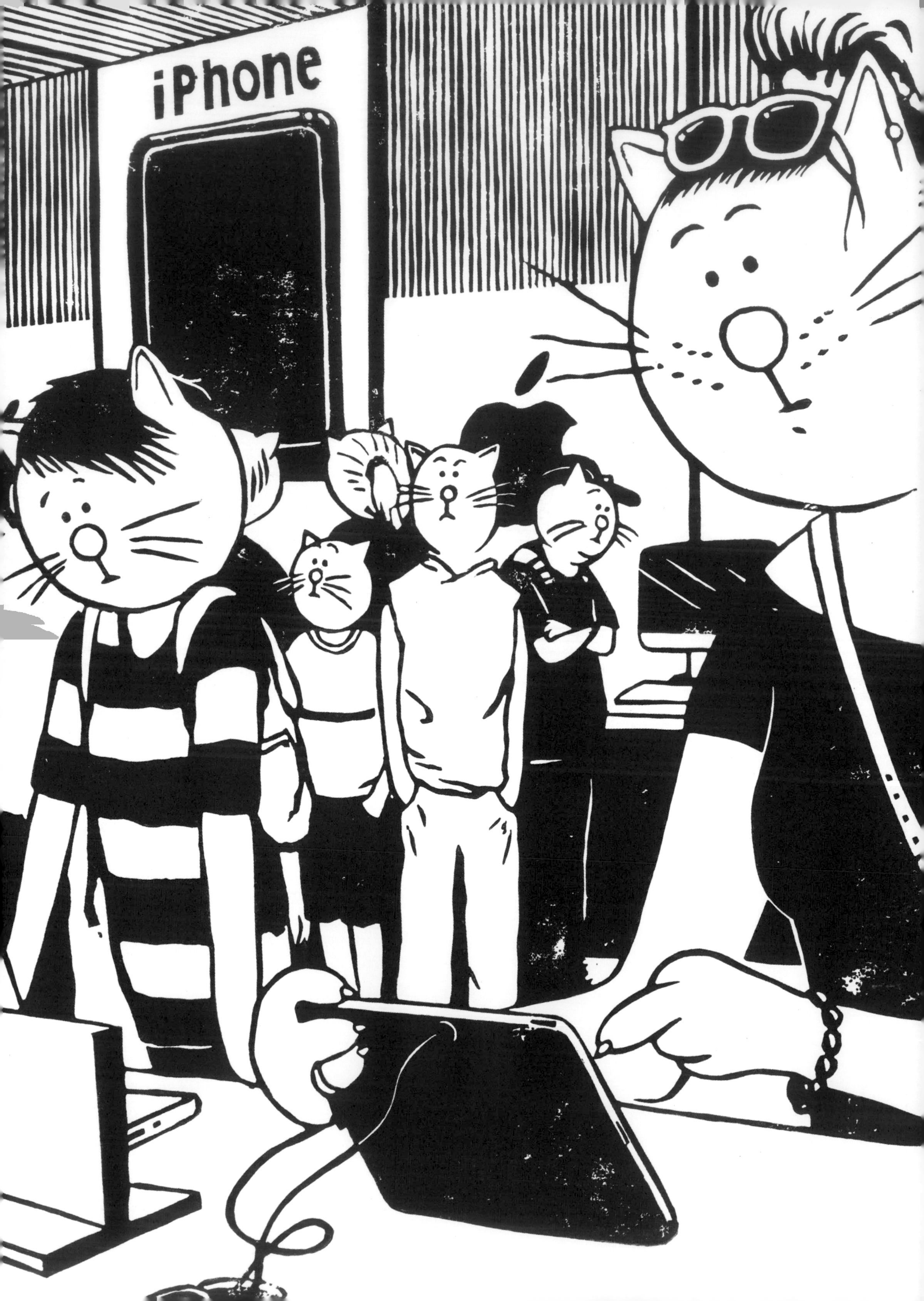
iPhone

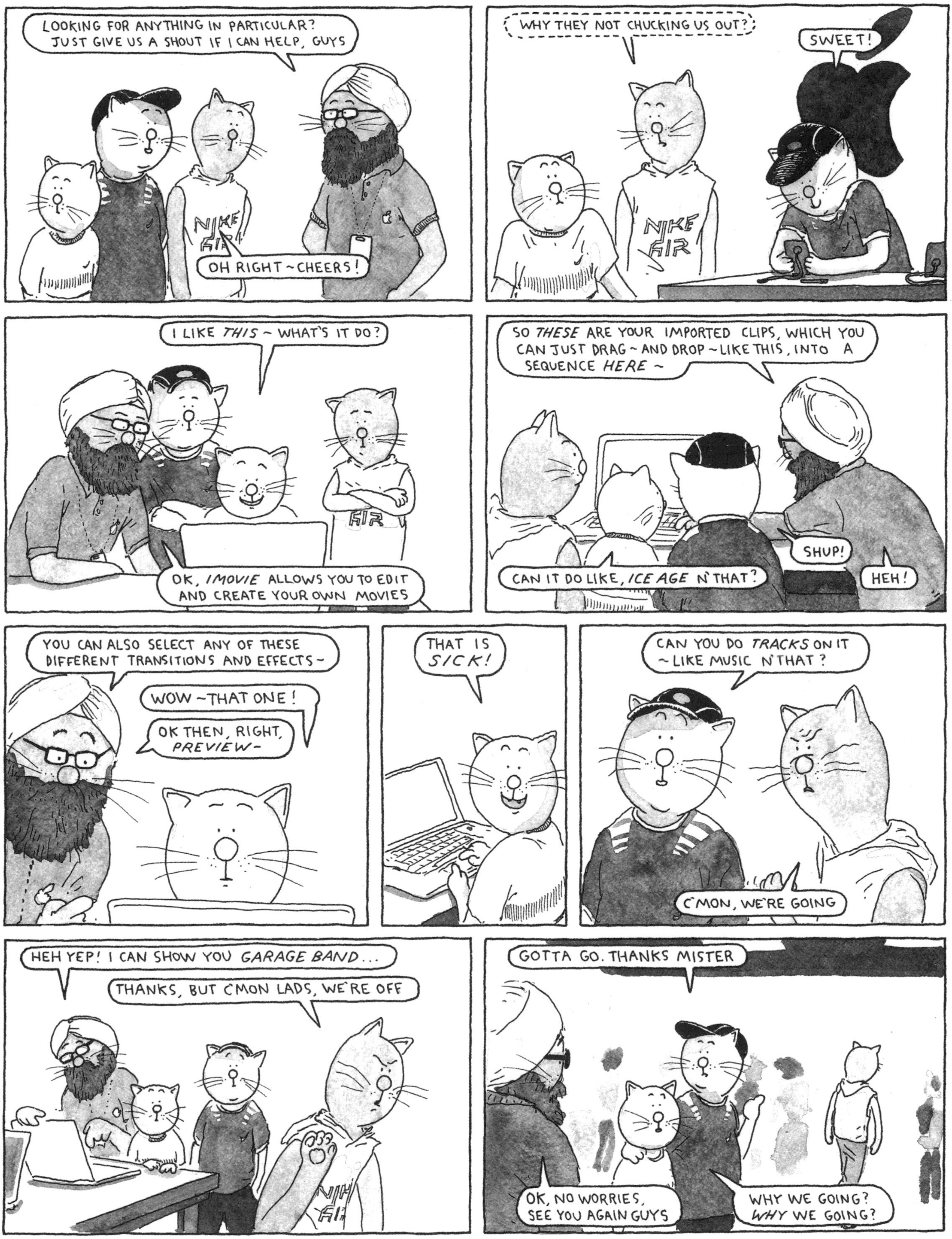
LOOKING FOR ANYTHING IN PARTICULAR? JUST GIVE US A SHOUT IF I CAN HELP, GUYS
OH RIGHT ~ CHEERS!
WHY THEY NOT CHUCKING US OUT?
SWEET!
I LIKE THIS ~ WHAT'S IT DO?
OK, IMOVIE ALLOWS YOU TO EDIT AND CREATE YOUR OWN MOVIES
SO THESE ARE YOUR IMPORTED CLIPS, WHICH YOU CAN JUST DRAG ~ AND DROP ~ LIKE THIS, INTO A SEQUENCE HERE ~
CAN IT DO LIKE, ICE AGE N'THAT?
SHUP!
HEH!
YOU CAN ALSO SELECT ANY OF THESE DIFFERENT TRANSITIONS AND EFFECTS ~
WOW ~ THAT ONE!
OK THEN, RIGHT, PREVIEW ~
THAT IS SICK!
CAN YOU DO TRACKS ON IT ~ LIKE MUSIC N'THAT?
C'MON, WE'RE GOING
HEH YEP! I CAN SHOW YOU GARAGE BAND ...
THANKS, BUT C'MON LADS, WE'RE OFF
GOTTA GO. THANKS MISTER
OK, NO WORRIES, SEE YOU AGAIN GUYS
WHY WE GOING? WHY WE GOING?

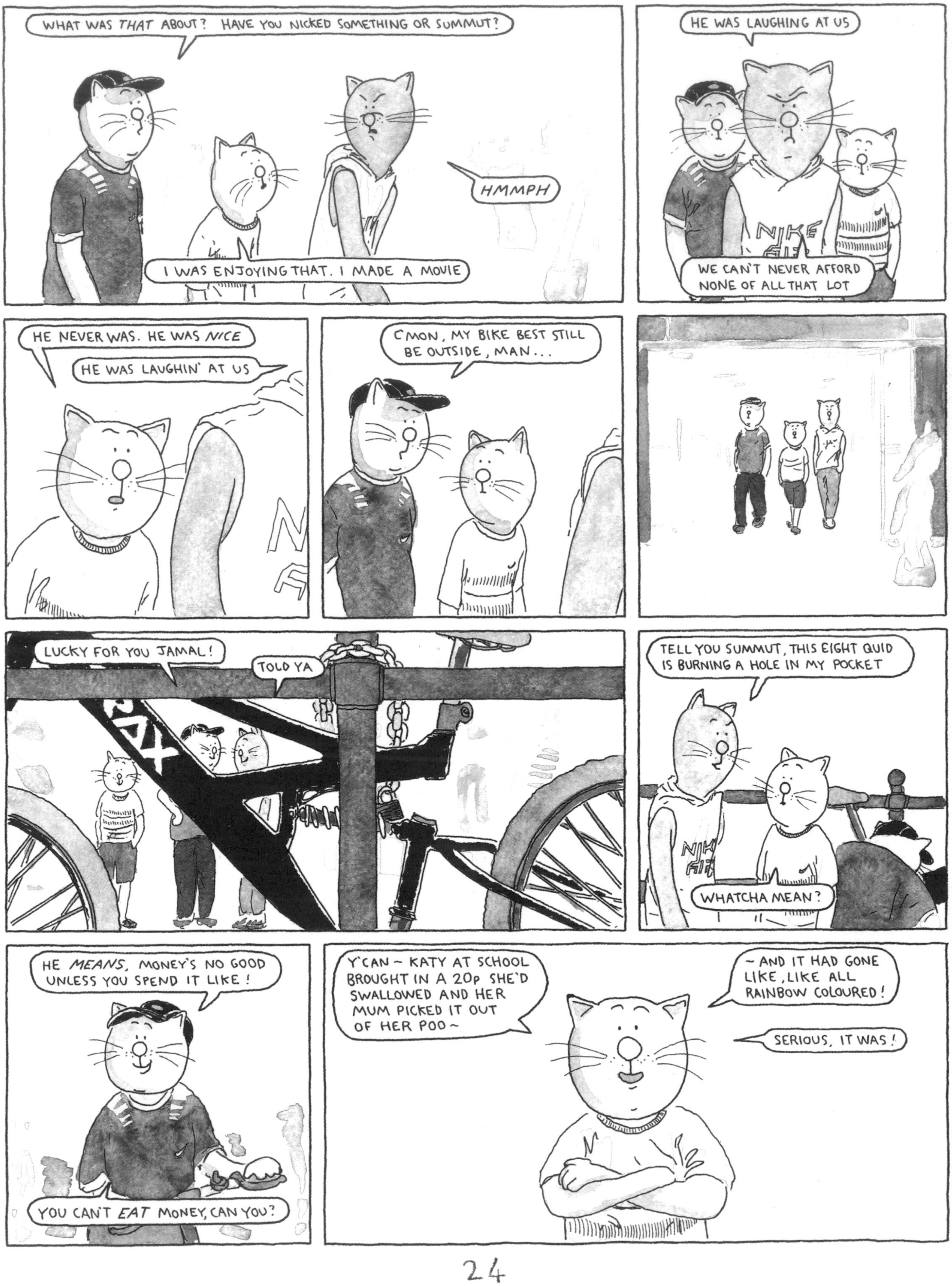

WHAT WAS THAT ABOUT? HAVE YOU NICKED SOMETHING OR SUMMUT?
HMMPH
I WAS ENJOYING THAT. I MADE A MOVIE
HE WAS LAUGHING AT US
WE CAN'T NEVER AFFORD NONE OF ALL THAT LOT
HE NEVER WAS. HE WAS NICE
HE WAS LAUGHIN' AT US
C'MON, MY BIKE BEST STILL BE OUTSIDE, MAN...
LUCKY FOR YOU JAMAL!
TOLD YA
TELL YOU SUMMUT, THIS EIGHT QUID IS BURNING A HOLE IN MY POCKET
WHATCHA MEAN?
HE MEANS, MONEY'S NO GOOD UNLESS YOU SPEND IT LIKE!
YOU CAN'T EAT MONEY, CAN YOU?
Y'CAN ~ KATY AT SCHOOL BROUGHT IN A 20p SHE'D SWALLOWED AND HER MUM PICKED IT OUT OF HER POO ~
~ AND IT HAD GONE LIKE, LIKE ALL RAINBOW COLOURED!
SERIOUS, IT WAS!

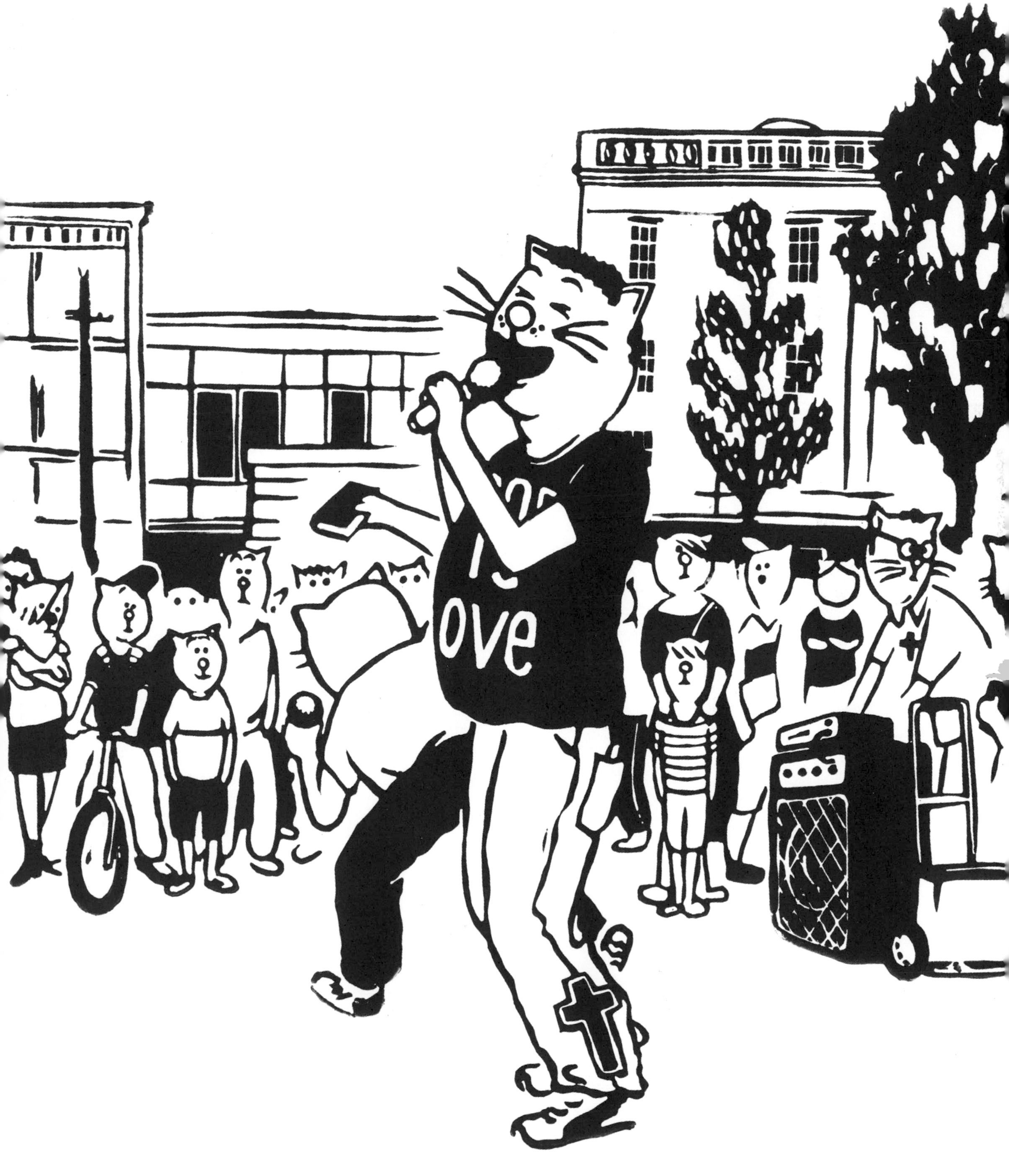

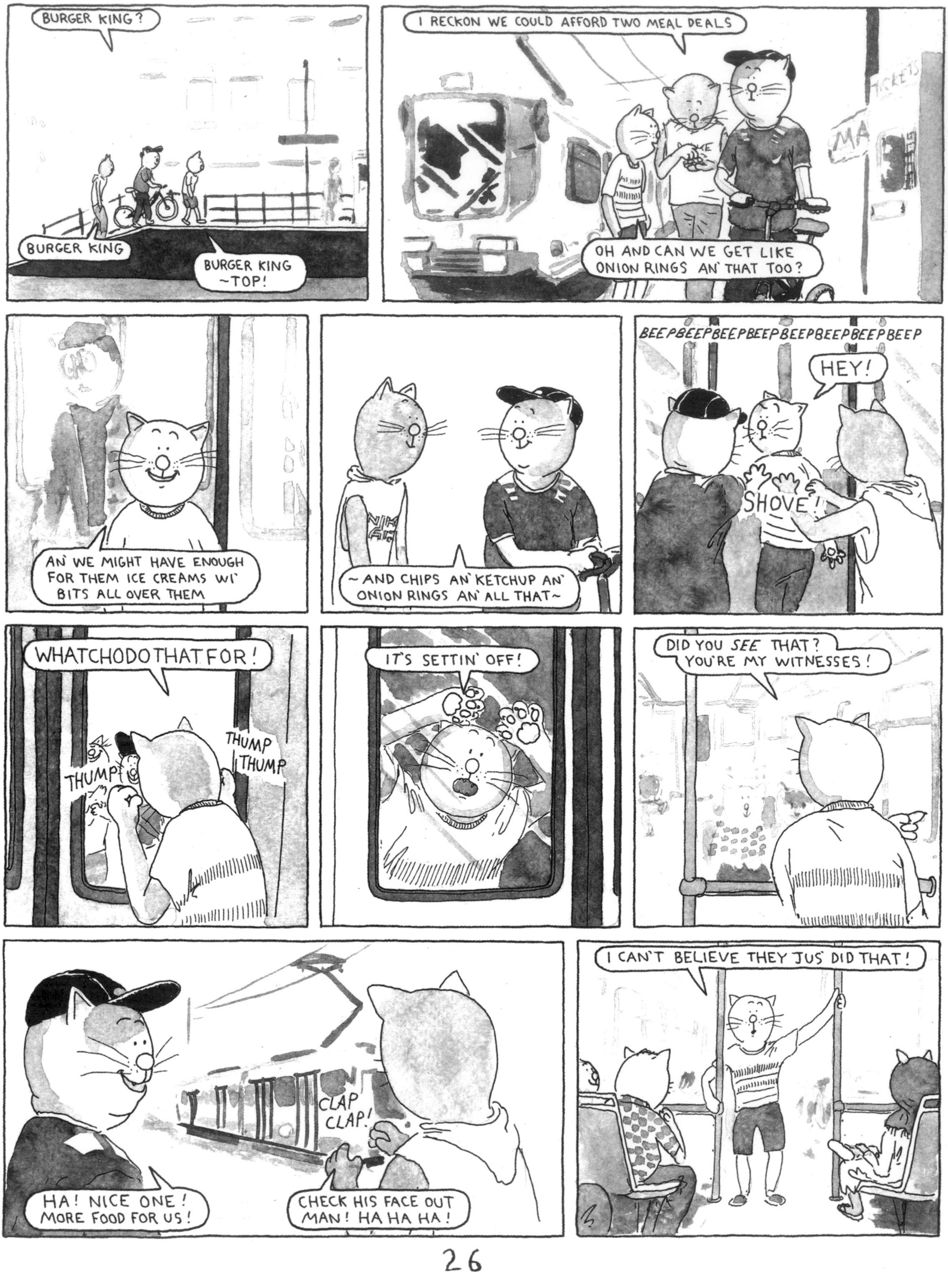
BURGER KING?
BURGER KING
BURGER KING ~TOP!
I RECKON WE COULD AFFORD TWO MEAL DEALS
OH AND CAN WE GET LIKE ONION RINGS AN' THAT TOO?
AN' WE MIGHT HAVE ENOUGH FOR THEM ICE CREAMS WI' BITS ALL OVER THEM
~AND CHIPS AN' KETCHUP AN' ONION RINGS AN' ALL THAT~
BEEPBEEPBEEPBEEPBEEPBEEPBEEPBEEP
HEY!
SHOVE!
WHATCHODOTHATFOR!
THUMP
THUMP THUMP
IT'S SETTIN' OFF!
DID YOU SEE THAT? YOU'RE MY WITNESSES!
HA! NICE ONE! MORE FOOD FOR US!
CLAP CLAP!
CHECK HIS FACE OUT MAN! HA HA HA!
I CAN'T BELIEVE THEY JUS' DID THAT!

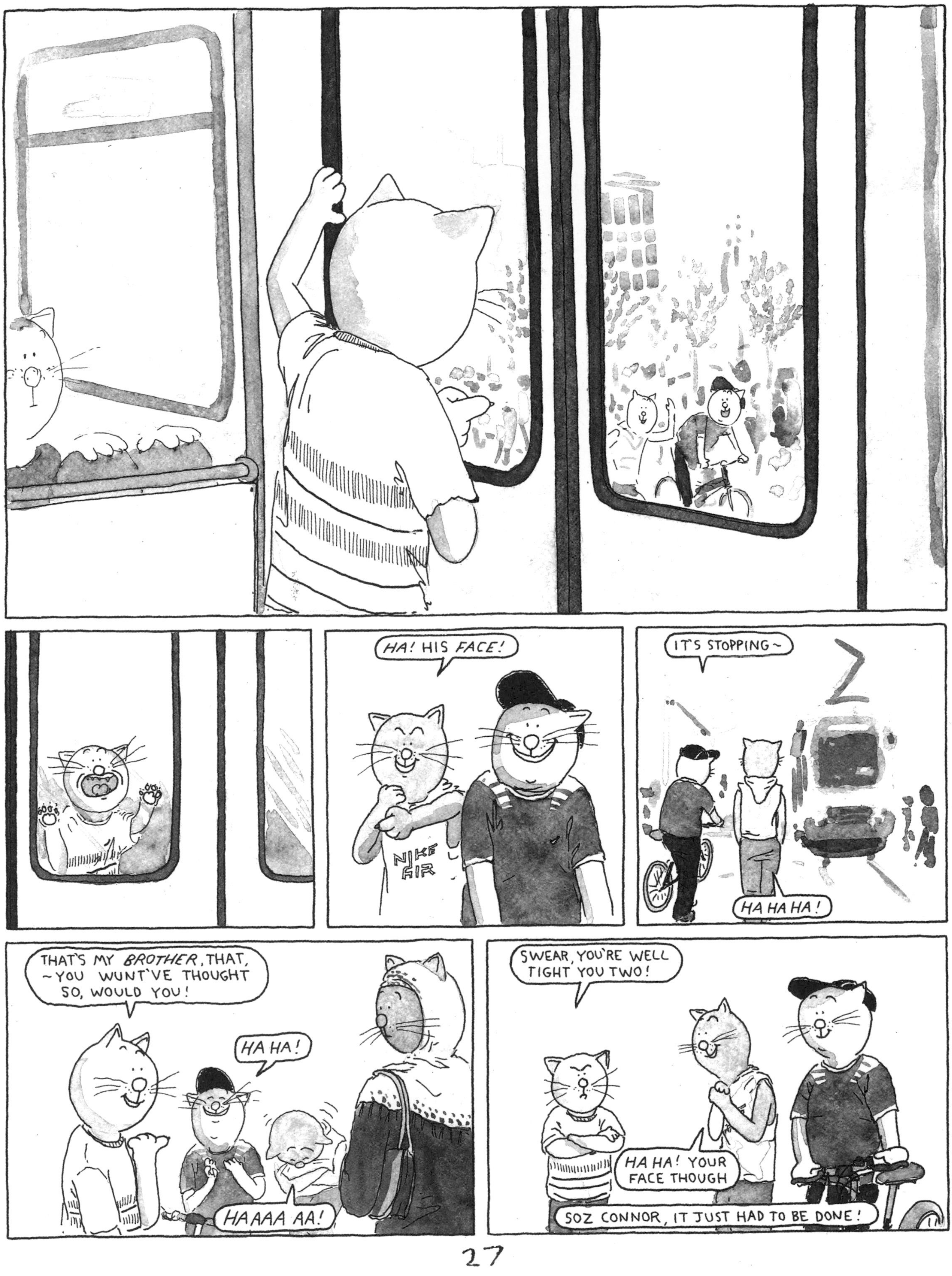

HA! HIS FACE!
IT'S STOPPING~
NIKE AIR
HA HA HA!
THAT'S MY BROTHER, THAT, ~YOU WUNT'VE THOUGHT SO, WOULD YOU!
HA HA!
HAAAA AA!
SWEAR, YOU'RE WELL TIGHT YOU TWO!
HA HA! YOUR FACE THOUGH
SOZ CONNOR, IT JUST HAD TO BE DONE!

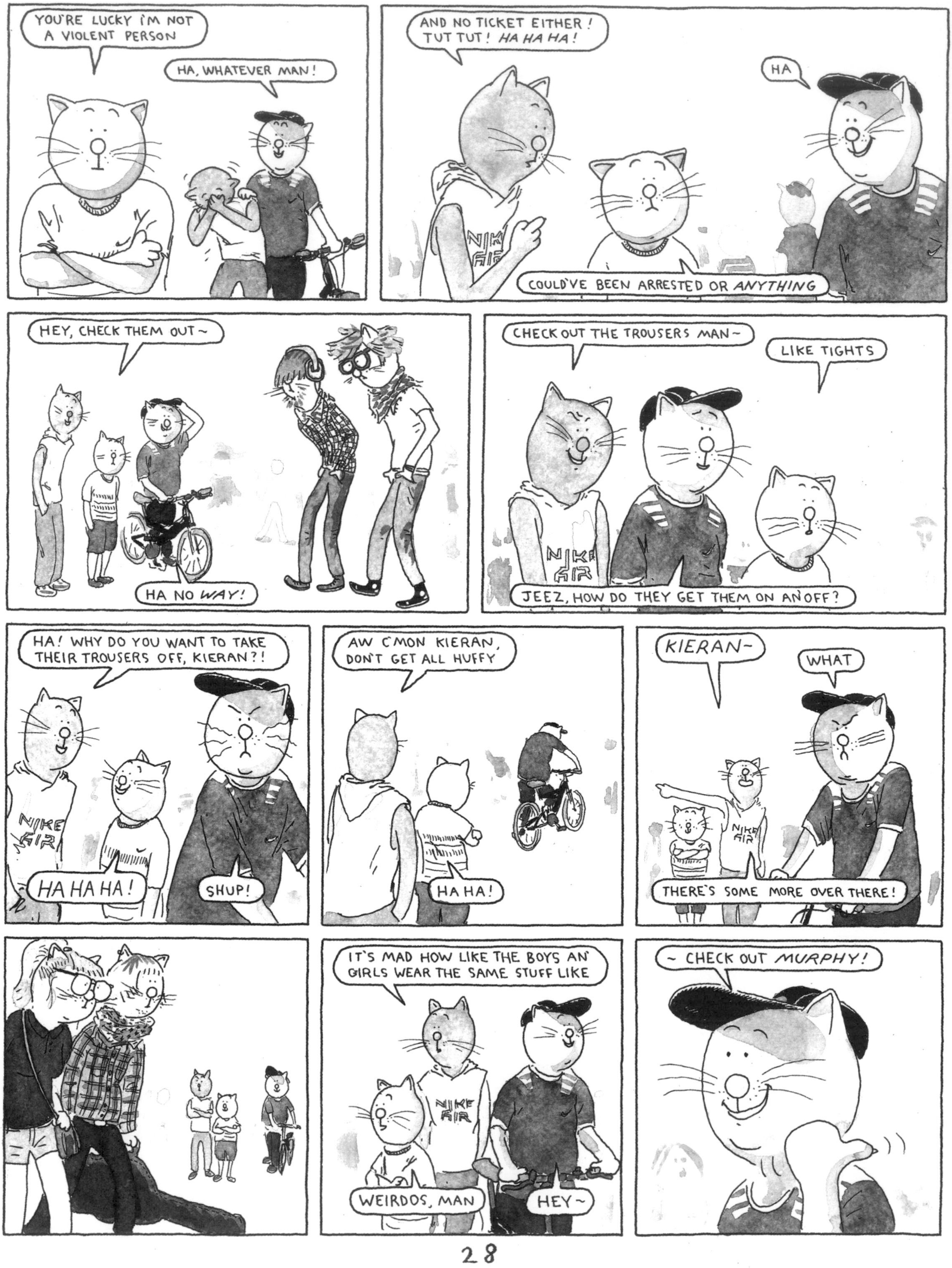
YOU'RE LUCKY I'M NOT A VIOLENT PERSON
HA, WHATEVER MAN!
AND NO TICKET EITHER! TUT TUT! HA HA HA!
HA
COULD'VE BEEN ARRESTED OR ANYTHING
HEY, CHECK THEM OUT~
HA NO WAY!
CHECK OUT THE TROUSERS MAN~
LIKE TIGHTS
JEEZ, HOW DO THEY GET THEM ON AN' OFF?
HA! WHY DO YOU WANT TO TAKE THEIR TROUSERS OFF, KIERAN?!
HA HA HA!
SHUP!
AW C'MON KIERAN, DON'T GET ALL HUFFY
HA HA!
KIERAN~
WHAT
THERE'S SOME MORE OVER THERE!
IT'S MAD HOW LIKE THE BOYS AN' GIRLS WEAR THE SAME STUFF LIKE
WEIRDOS, MAN
HEY~
~ CHECK OUT MURPHY!

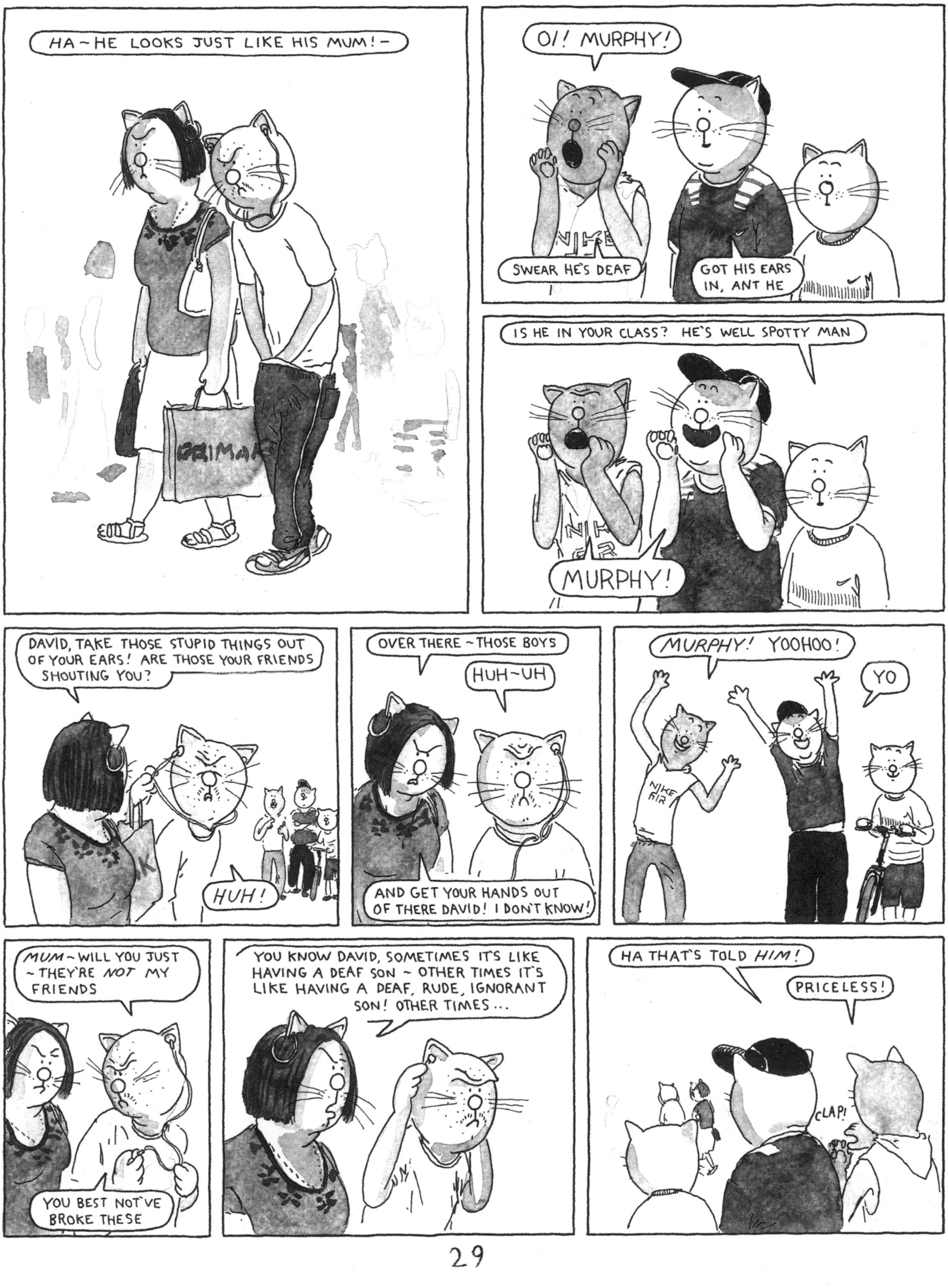
HA ~ HE LOOKS JUST LIKE HIS MUM! -
OI! MURPHY!
SWEAR HE'S DEAF
GOT HIS EARS IN, ANT HE
IS HE IN YOUR CLASS? HE'S WELL SPOTTY MAN
MURPHY!
DAVID, TAKE THOSE STUPID THINGS OUT OF YOUR EARS! ARE THOSE YOUR FRIENDS SHOUTING YOU?
HUH!
OVER THERE ~ THOSE BOYS
HUH ~ UH
AND GET YOUR HANDS OUT OF THERE DAVID! I DON'T KNOW!
MURPHY! YOOHOO!
YO
MUM ~ WILL YOU JUST ~ THEY'RE NOT MY FRIENDS
YOU BEST NOT'VE BROKE THESE
YOU KNOW DAVID, SOMETIMES IT'S LIKE HAVING A DEAF SON ~ OTHER TIMES IT'S LIKE HAVING A DEAF, RUDE, IGNORANT SON! OTHER TIMES...
HA THAT'S TOLD HIM!
PRICELESS!
CLAP!

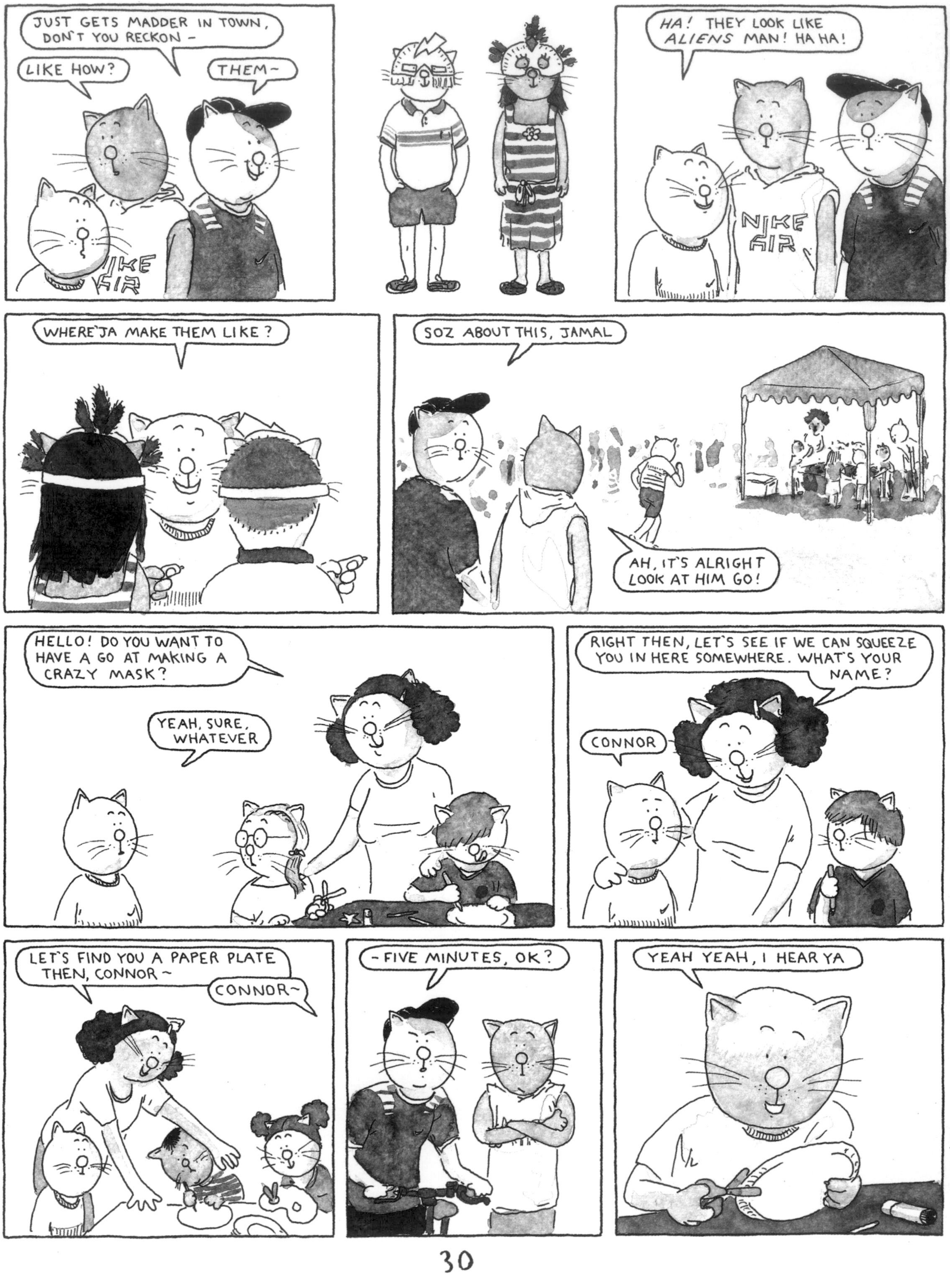
JUST GETS MADDER IN TOWN, DON'T YOU RECKON -
LIKE HOW?
THEM-
HA! THEY LOOK LIKE ALIENS MAN! HA HA!
NIKE AIR
WHERE'JA MAKE THEM LIKE?
SOZ ABOUT THIS, JAMAL
AH, IT'S ALRIGHT LOOK AT HIM GO!
HELLO! DO YOU WANT TO HAVE A GO AT MAKING A CRAZY MASK?
YEAH, SURE, WHATEVER
RIGHT THEN, LET'S SEE IF WE CAN SQUEEZE YOU IN HERE SOMEWHERE. WHAT'S YOUR NAME?
CONNOR
LET'S FIND YOU A PAPER PLATE THEN, CONNOR~
CONNOR~
-FIVE MINUTES, OK?
YEAH YEAH, I HEAR YA

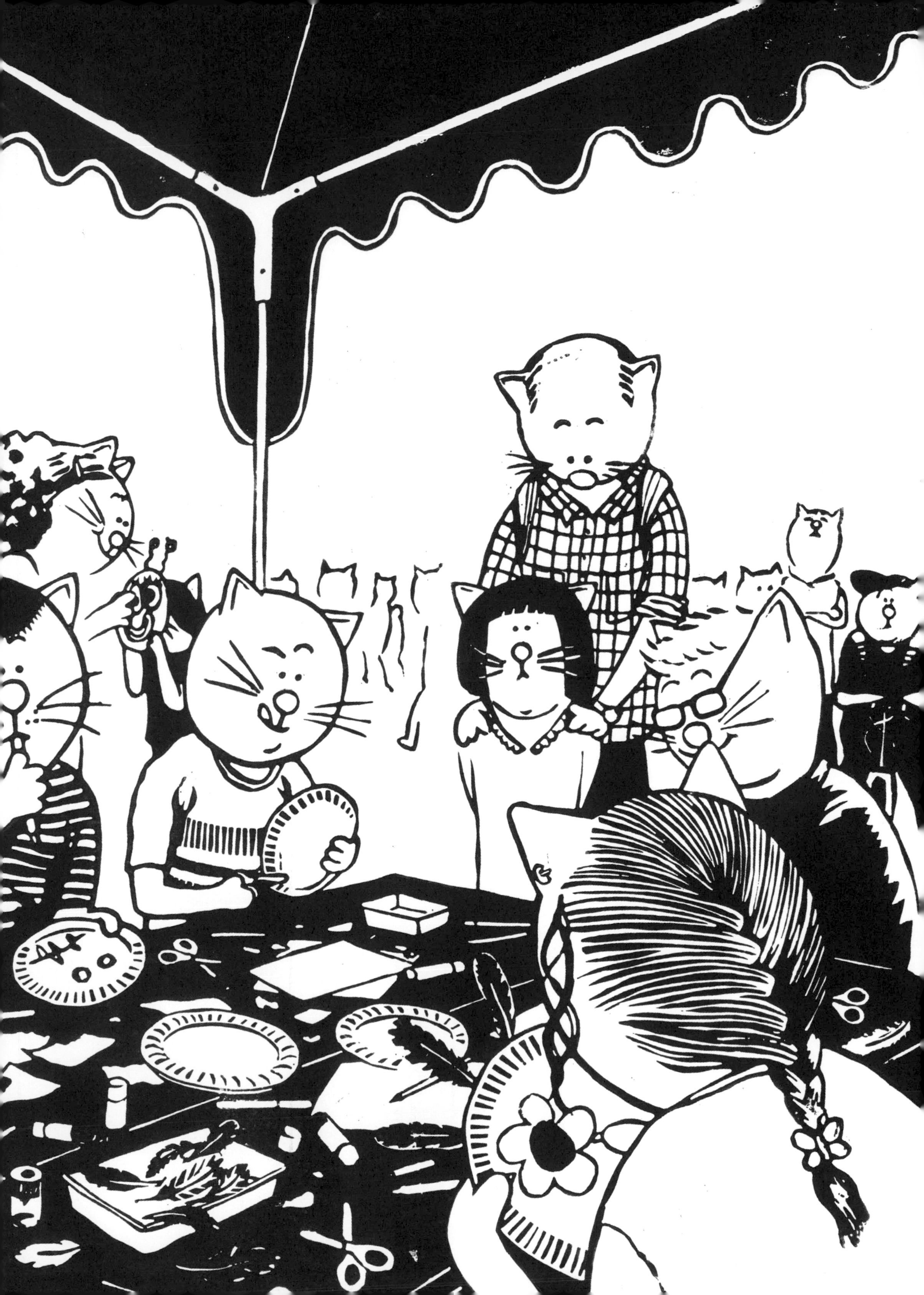

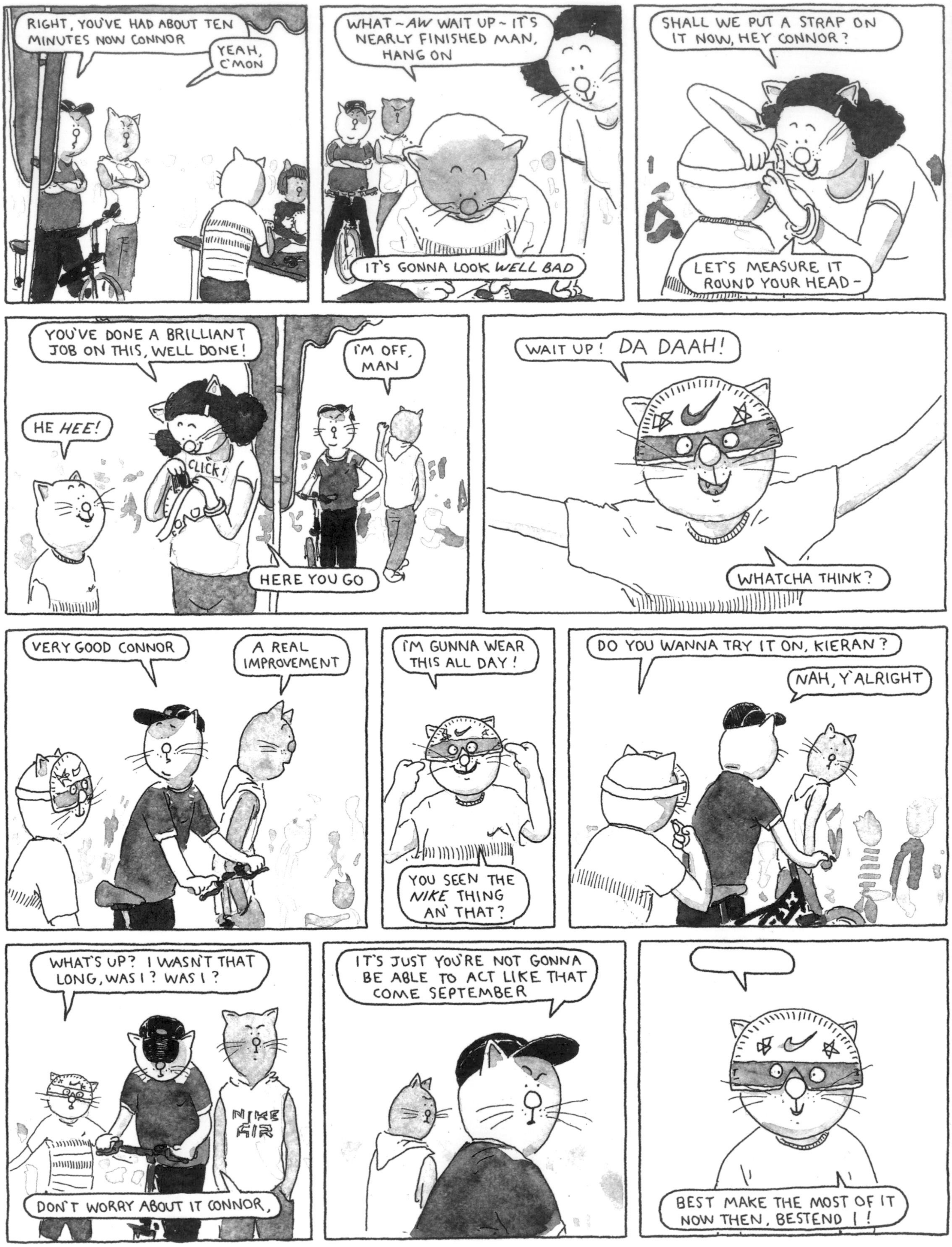
RIGHT, YOU'VE HAD ABOUT TEN MINUTES NOW CONNOR
YEAH, C'MON
WHAT ~ AW WAIT UP ~ IT'S NEARLY FINISHED MAN, HANG ON
IT'S GONNA LOOK WELL BAD
SHALL WE PUT A STRAP ON IT NOW, HEY CONNOR?
LET'S MEASURE IT ROUND YOUR HEAD -
YOU'VE DONE A BRILLIANT JOB ON THIS, WELL DONE!
HE HEE!
CLICK!
I'M OFF, MAN
HERE YOU GO
WAIT UP! DA DAAH!
WHATCHA THINK?
VERY GOOD CONNOR
A REAL IMPROVEMENT
I'M GUNNA WEAR THIS ALL DAY!
YOU SEEN THE NIKE THING AN' THAT?
DO YOU WANNA TRY IT ON, KIERAN?
NAH, Y'ALRIGHT
WHAT'S UP? I WASN'T THAT LONG, WAS I? WAS I?
NIKE AIR
DON'T WORRY ABOUT IT CONNOR,
IT'S JUST YOU'RE NOT GONNA BE ABLE TO ACT LIKE THAT COME SEPTEMBER
BEST MAKE THE MOST OF IT NOW THEN, BESTEND!!

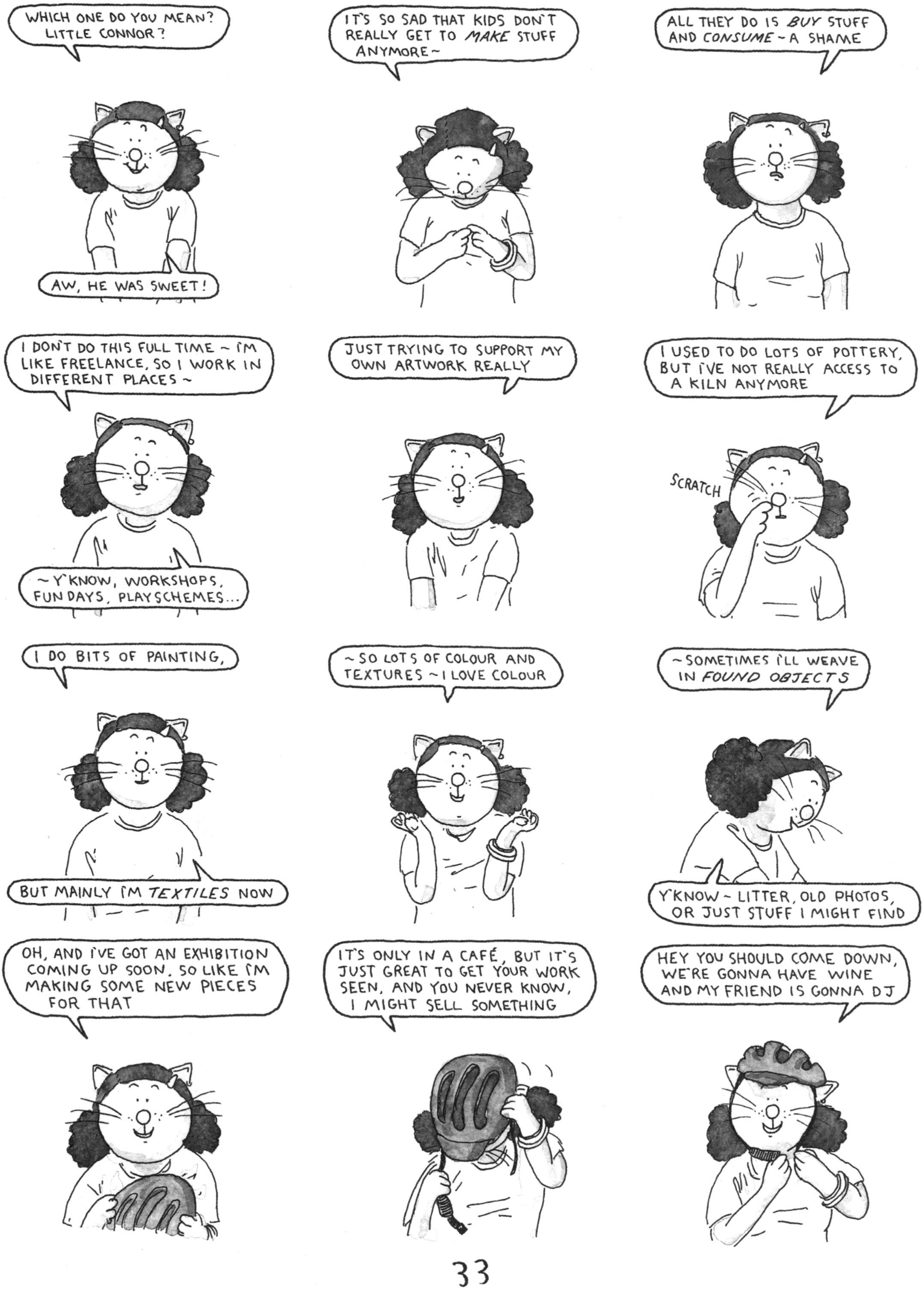
WHICH ONE DO YOU MEAN? LITTLE CONNOR?
AW, HE WAS SWEET!
IT'S SO SAD THAT KIDS DON'T REALLY GET TO *MAKE* STUFF ANYMORE~
ALL THEY DO IS *BUY* STUFF AND *CONSUME* ~ A SHAME
I DON'T DO THIS FULL TIME ~ I'M LIKE FREELANCE, SO I WORK IN DIFFERENT PLACES ~
~ Y'KNOW, WORKSHOPS, FUN DAYS, PLAYSCHEMES...
JUST TRYING TO SUPPORT MY OWN ARTWORK REALLY
I USED TO DO LOTS OF POTTERY, BUT I'VE NOT REALLY ACCESS TO A KILN ANYMORE
SCRATCH
I DO BITS OF PAINTING,
BUT MAINLY I'M *TEXTILES* NOW
~ SO LOTS OF COLOUR AND TEXTURES ~ I LOVE COLOUR
~ SOMETIMES I'LL WEAVE IN *FOUND OBJECTS*
Y'KNOW ~ LITTER, OLD PHOTOS, OR JUST STUFF I MIGHT FIND
OH, AND I'VE GOT AN EXHIBITION COMING UP SOON. SO LIKE I'M MAKING SOME NEW PIECES FOR THAT
IT'S ONLY IN A CAFÉ, BUT IT'S JUST GREAT TO GET YOUR WORK SEEN, AND YOU NEVER KNOW, I MIGHT SELL SOMETHING
HEY YOU SHOULD COME DOWN, WE'RE GONNA HAVE WINE AND MY FRIEND IS GONNA DJ

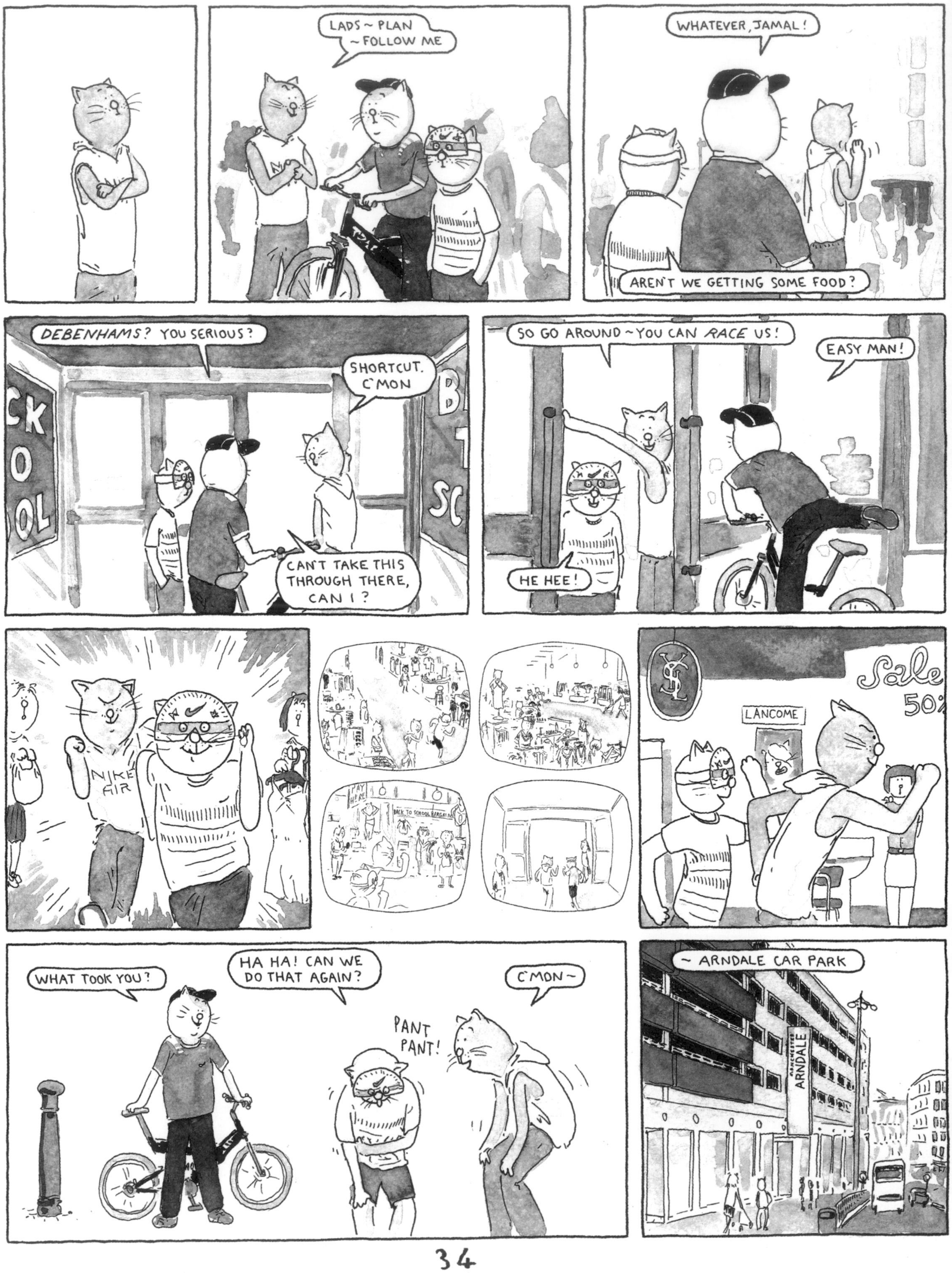
LADS ~ PLAN ~ FOLLOW ME
WHATEVER, JAMAL!
AREN'T WE GETTING SOME FOOD?
DEBENHAMS? YOU SERIOUS?
SHORTCUT. C'MON
CAN'T TAKE THIS THROUGH THERE, CAN I?
SO GO AROUND ~ YOU CAN RACE US!
EASY MAN!
HE HEE!
NIKE AIR
Sale
50%
LANCOME
WHAT TOOK YOU?
HA HA! CAN WE DO THAT AGAIN?
C'MON ~
PANT PANT!
~ ARNDALE CAR PARK
MANCHESTER
ARNDALE

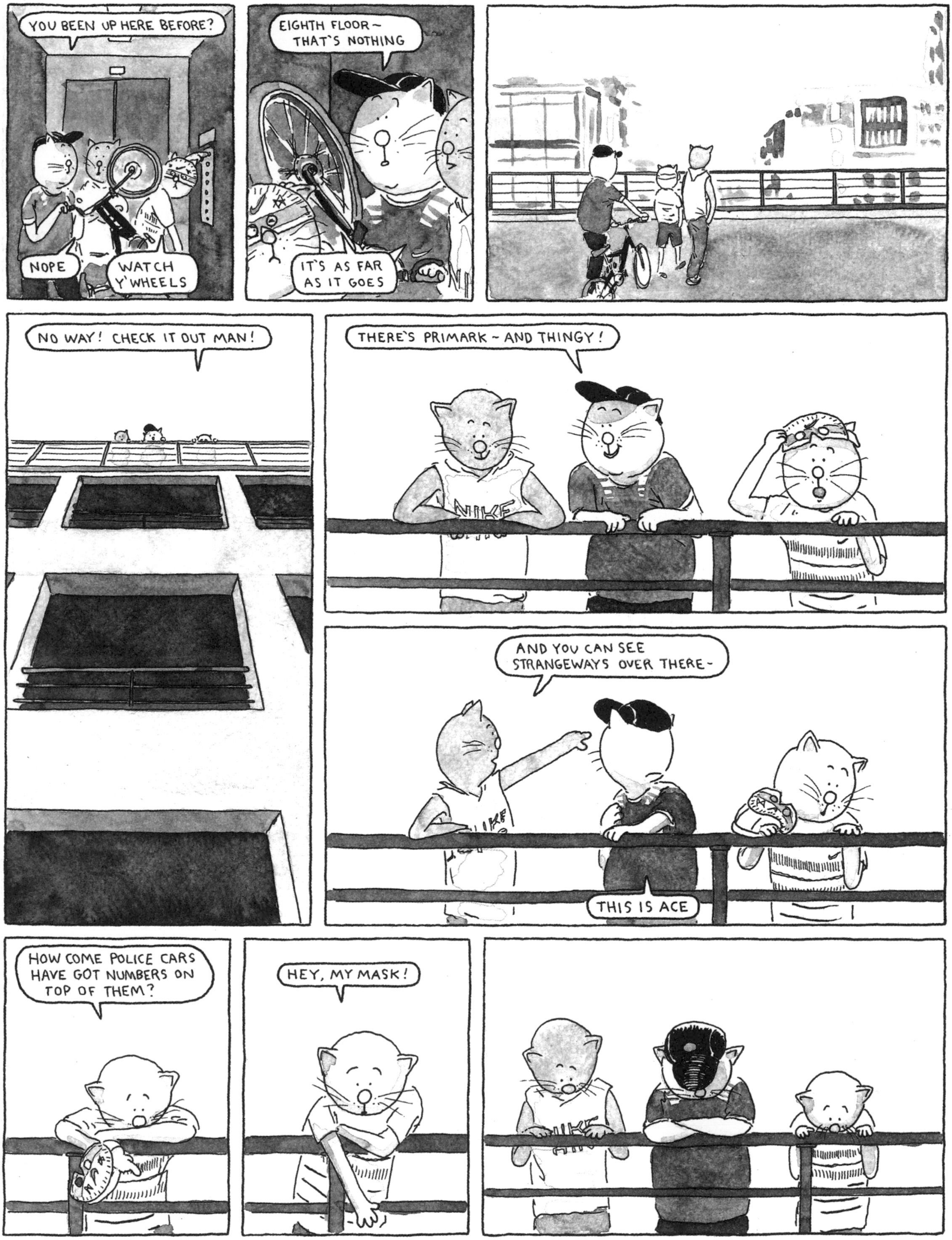
YOU BEEN UP HERE BEFORE?
NOPE
WATCH Y'WHEELS
EIGHTH FLOOR ~ THAT'S NOTHING
IT'S AS FAR AS IT GOES
NO WAY! CHECK IT OUT MAN!
THERE'S PRIMARK ~ AND THINGY!
AND YOU CAN SEE STRANGEWAYS OVER THERE ~
THIS IS ACE
HOW COME POLICE CARS HAVE GOT NUMBERS ON TOP OF THEM?
HEY, MY MASK!

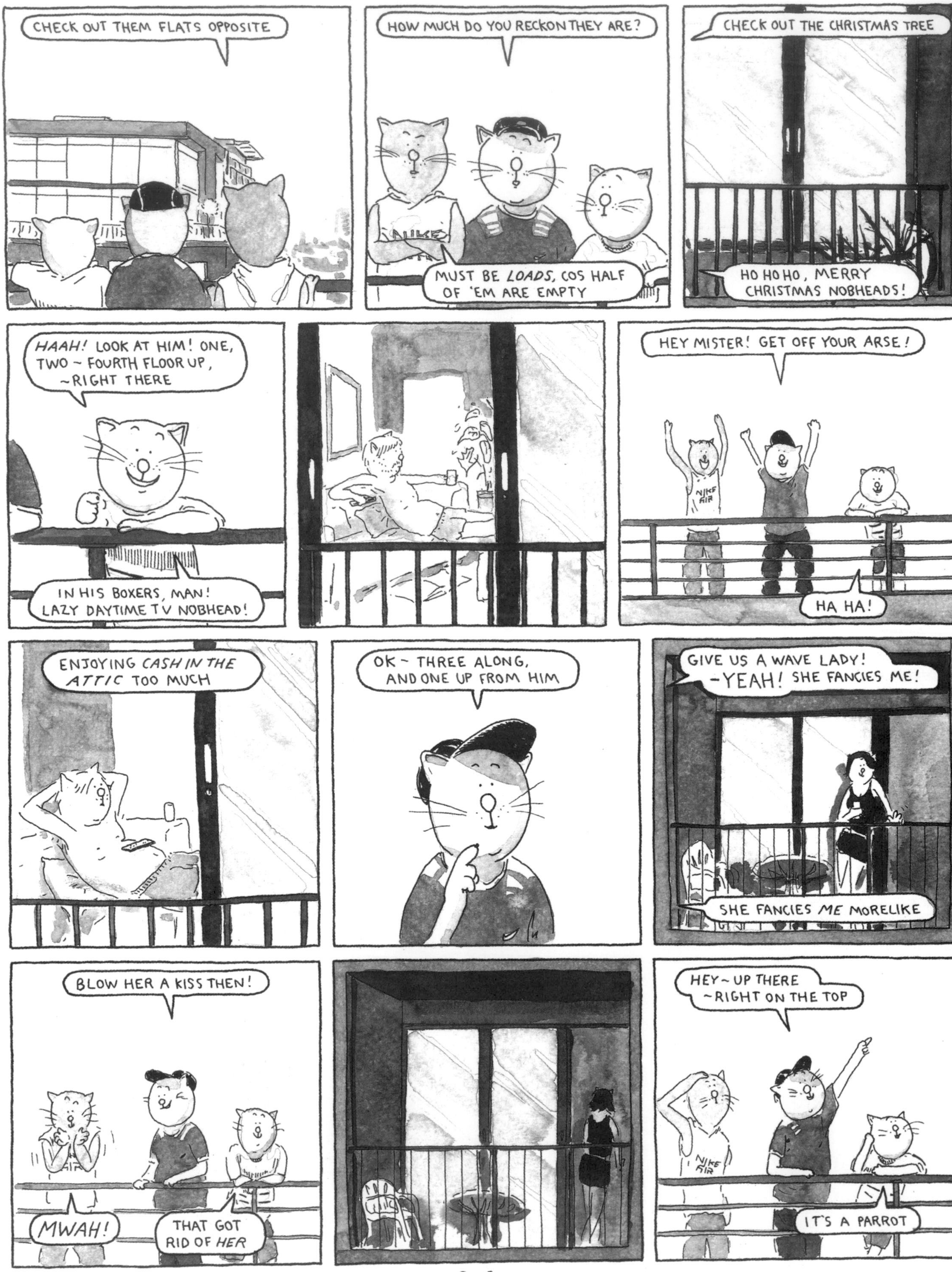
CHECK OUT THEM FLATS OPPOSITE
HOW MUCH DO YOU RECKON THEY ARE?
MUST BE LOADS, COS HALF OF 'EM ARE EMPTY
CHECK OUT THE CHRISTMAS TREE
HO HO HO, MERRY CHRISTMAS NOBHEADS!
HAAH! LOOK AT HIM! ONE, TWO ~ FOURTH FLOOR UP, ~RIGHT THERE
IN HIS BOXERS, MAN! LAZY DAYTIME TV NOBHEAD!
HEY MISTER! GET OFF YOUR ARSE!
HA HA!
ENJOYING CASH IN THE ATTIC TOO MUCH
OK ~ THREE ALONG, AND ONE UP FROM HIM
GIVE US A WAVE LADY!
-YEAH! SHE FANCIES ME!
SHE FANCIES ME MORELIKE
BLOW HER A KISS THEN!
MWAH!
THAT GOT RID OF HER
HEY ~ UP THERE ~RIGHT ON THE TOP
IT'S A PARROT

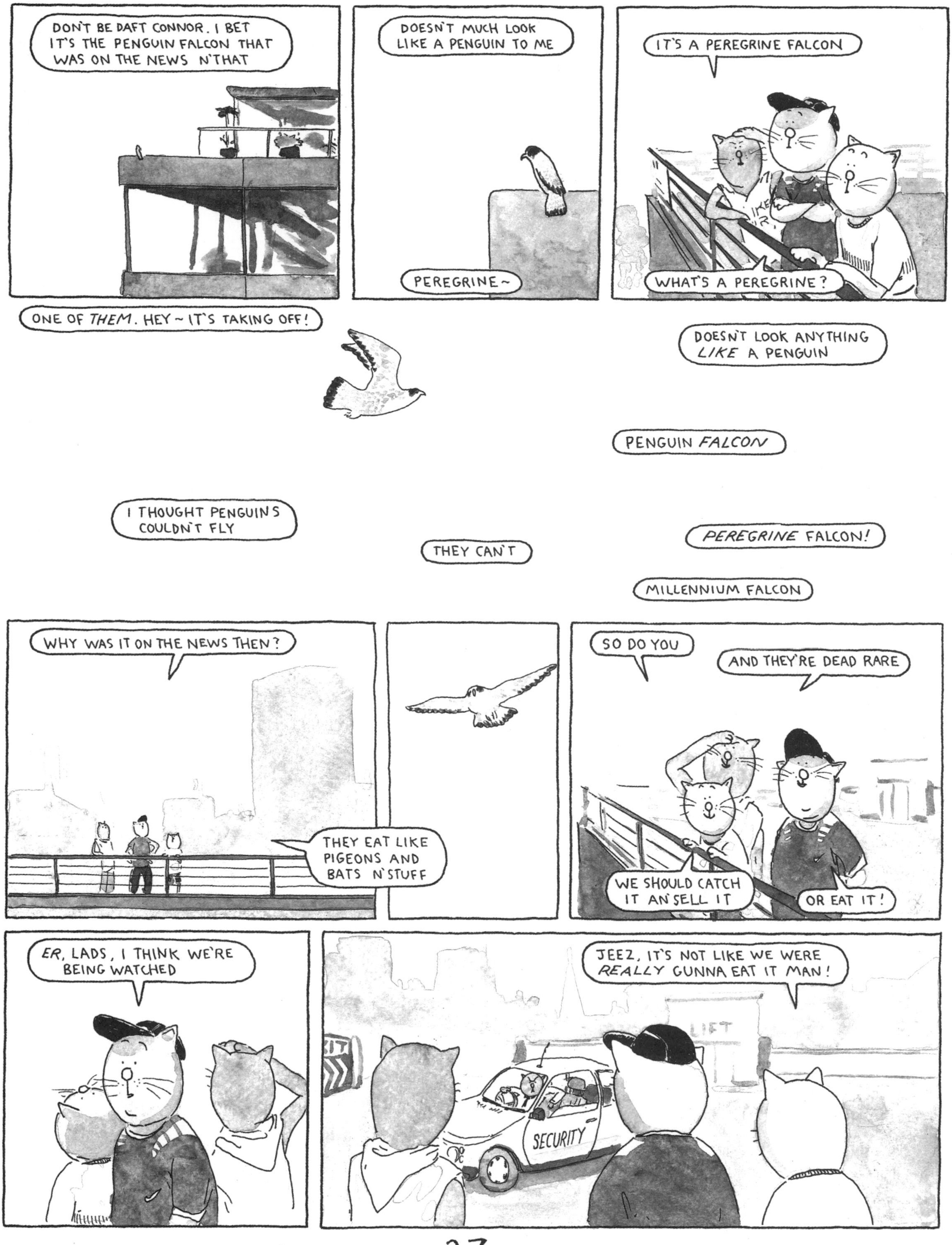
DON'T BE DAFT CONNOR. I BET IT'S THE PENGUIN FALCON THAT WAS ON THE NEWS N'THAT
DOESN'T MUCH LOOK LIKE A PENGUIN TO ME
PEREGRINE~
IT'S A PEREGRINE FALCON
WHAT'S A PEREGRINE?
ONE OF THEM. HEY ~ IT'S TAKING OFF!
DOESN'T LOOK ANYTHING LIKE A PENGUIN
PENGUIN FALCON
I THOUGHT PENGUINS COULDN'T FLY
THEY CAN'T
PEREGRINE FALCON!
MILLENNIUM FALCON
WHY WAS IT ON THE NEWS THEN?
THEY EAT LIKE PIGEONS AND BATS N'STUFF
SO DO YOU
AND THEY'RE DEAD RARE
WE SHOULD CATCH IT AN'SELL IT
OR EAT IT!
ER, LADS, I THINK WE'RE BEING WATCHED
JEEZ, IT'S NOT LIKE WE WERE REALLY GUNNA EAT IT MAN!
SECURITY

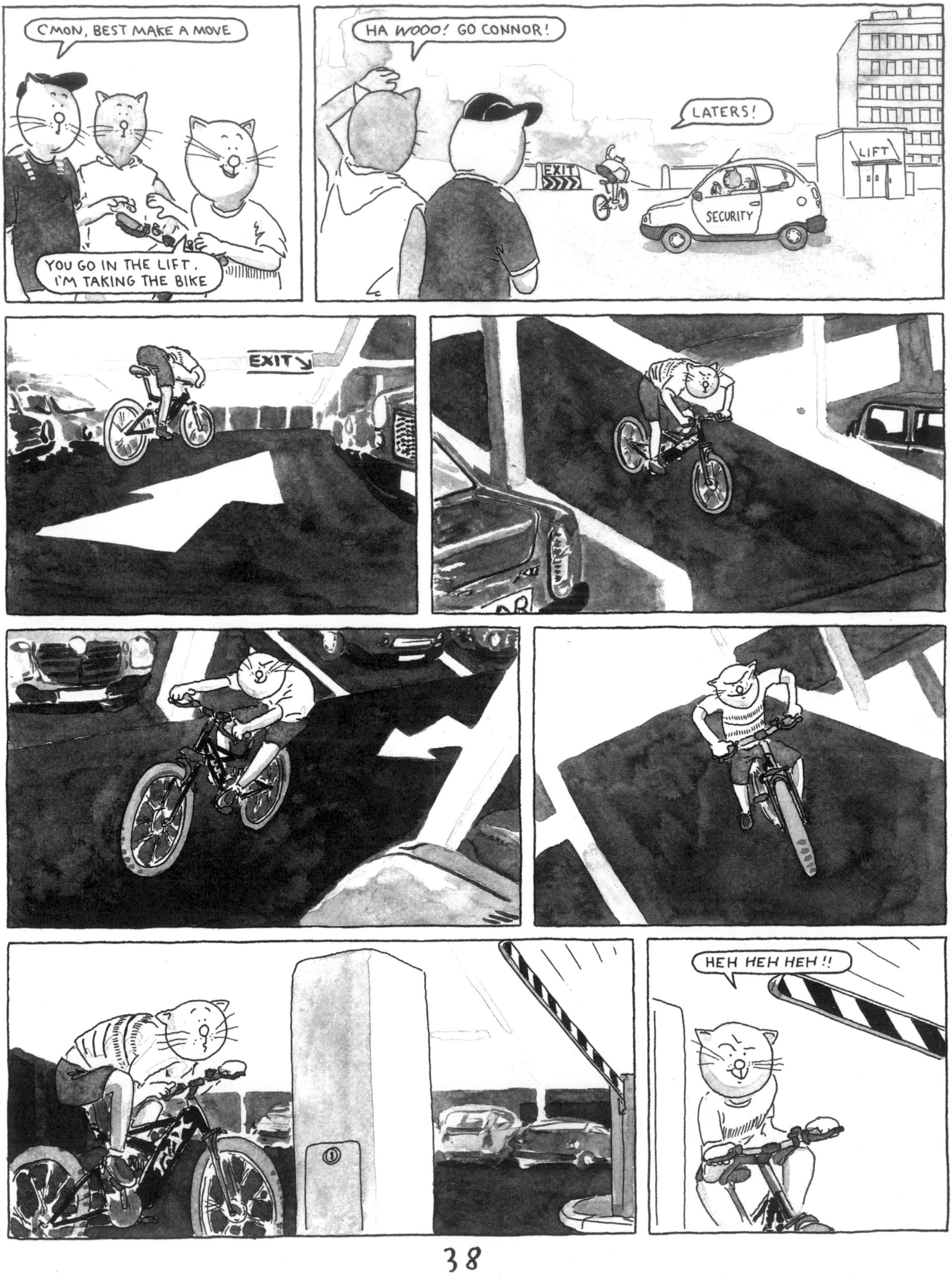
C'MON, BEST MAKE A MOVE
YOU GO IN THE LIFT, I'M TAKING THE BIKE
HA WOOO! GO CONNOR!
LATERS!
EXIT
LIFT
SECURITY
EXIT
HEH HEH HEH!!

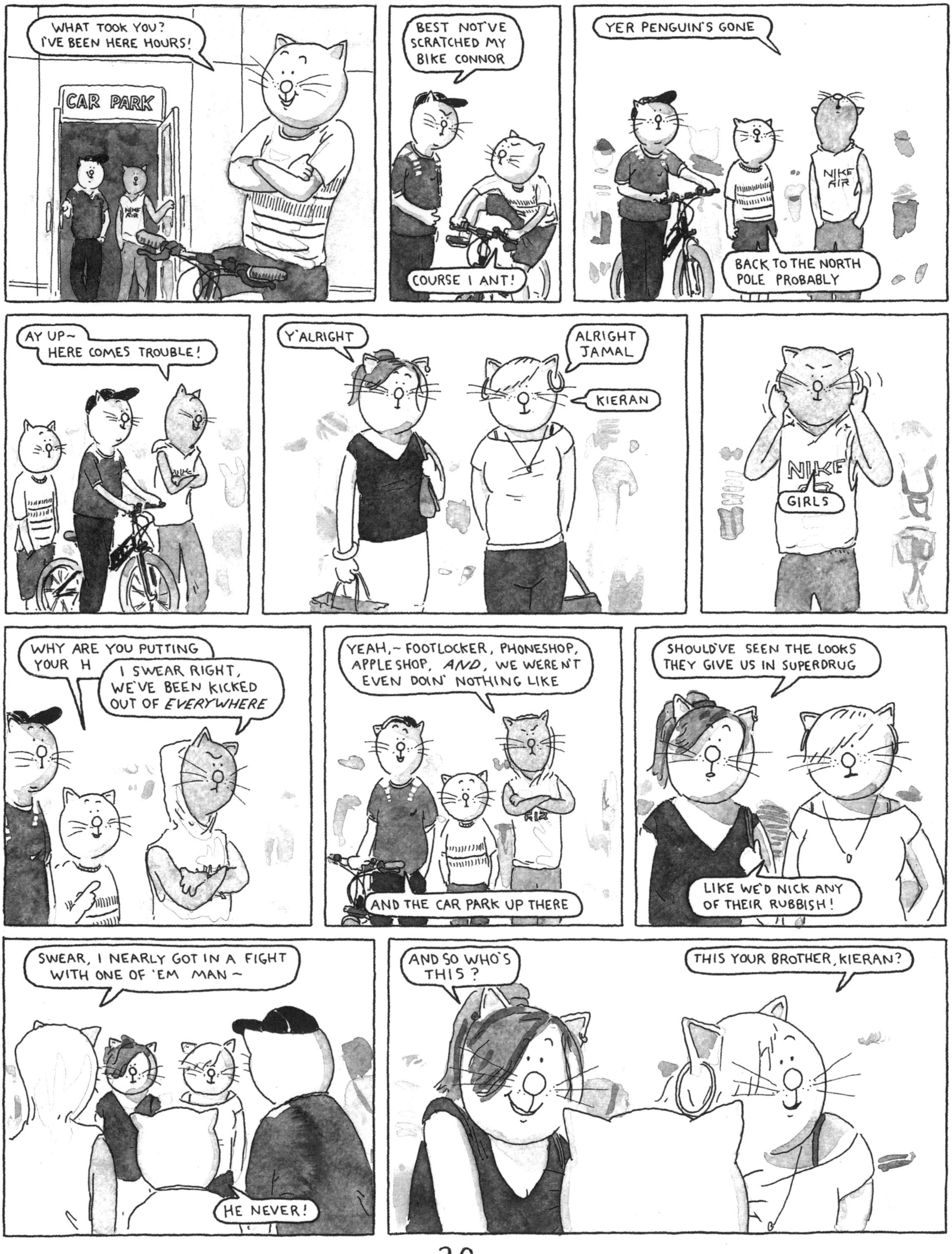
WHAT TOOK YOU? I'VE BEEN HERE HOURS!
CAR PARK
NIKE AIR
BEST NOT'VE SCRATCHED MY BIKE CONNOR
COURSE I ANT!
YER PENGUIN'S GONE
NIKE AIR
BACK TO THE NORTH POLE PROBABLY
AY UP~ HERE COMES TROUBLE!
Y'ALRIGHT
ALRIGHT JAMAL
KIERAN
NIKE
GIRLS
WHY ARE YOU PUTTING YOUR H
I SWEAR RIGHT, WE'VE BEEN KICKED OUT OF EVERYWHERE
YEAH,~ FOOTLOCKER, PHONESHOP, APPLE SHOP, AND, WE WEREN'T EVEN DOIN' NOTHING LIKE
AND THE CAR PARK UP THERE
SHOULD'VE SEEN THE LOOKS THEY GIVE US IN SUPERDRUG
LIKE WE'D NICK ANY OF THEIR RUBBISH!
SWEAR, I NEARLY GOT IN A FIGHT WITH ONE OF 'EM MAN~
HE NEVER!
AND SO WHO'S THIS?
THIS YOUR BROTHER, KIERAN?

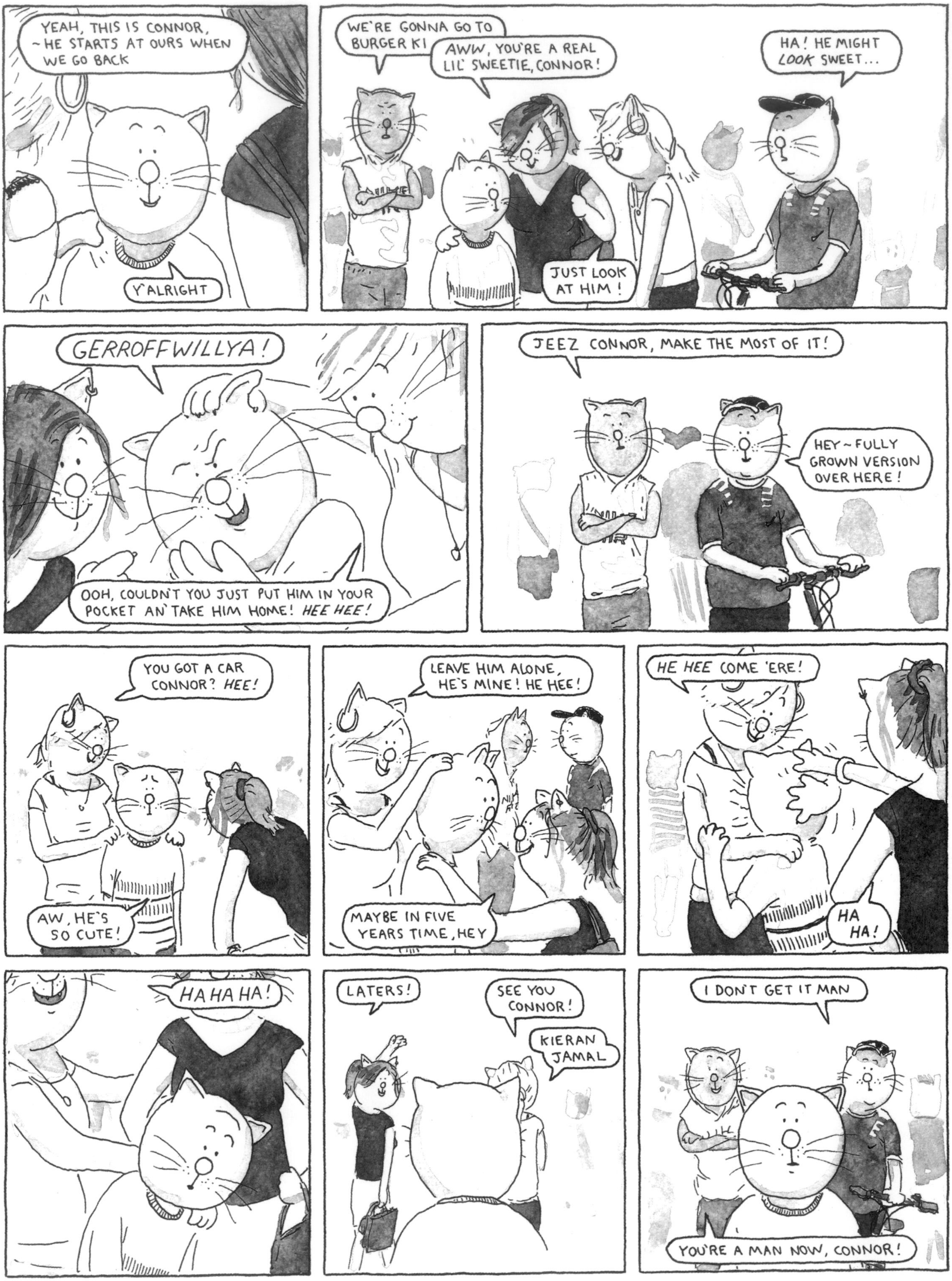
YEAH, THIS IS CONNOR, ~HE STARTS AT OURS WHEN WE GO BACK
Y'ALRIGHT
WE'RE GONNA GO TO BURGER KI
AWW, YOU'RE A REAL LIL' SWEETIE, CONNOR!
JUST LOOK AT HIM!
HA! HE MIGHT *LOOK* SWEET...
GERROFFWILLYA!
OOH, COULDN'T YOU JUST PUT HIM IN YOUR POCKET AN' TAKE HIM HOME! *HEE HEE!*
JEEZ CONNOR, MAKE THE MOST OF IT!
HEY ~ FULLY GROWN VERSION OVER HERE!
YOU GOT A CAR CONNOR? *HEE!*
AW, HE'S SO CUTE!
LEAVE HIM ALONE, HE'S MINE! HE HEE!
MAYBE IN FIVE YEARS TIME, HEY
HE HEE COME 'ERE!
HA HA!
HA HA HA!
LATERS!
SEE YOU CONNOR!
KIERAN JAMAL
I DON'T GET IT MAN
YOU'RE A MAN NOW, CONNOR!

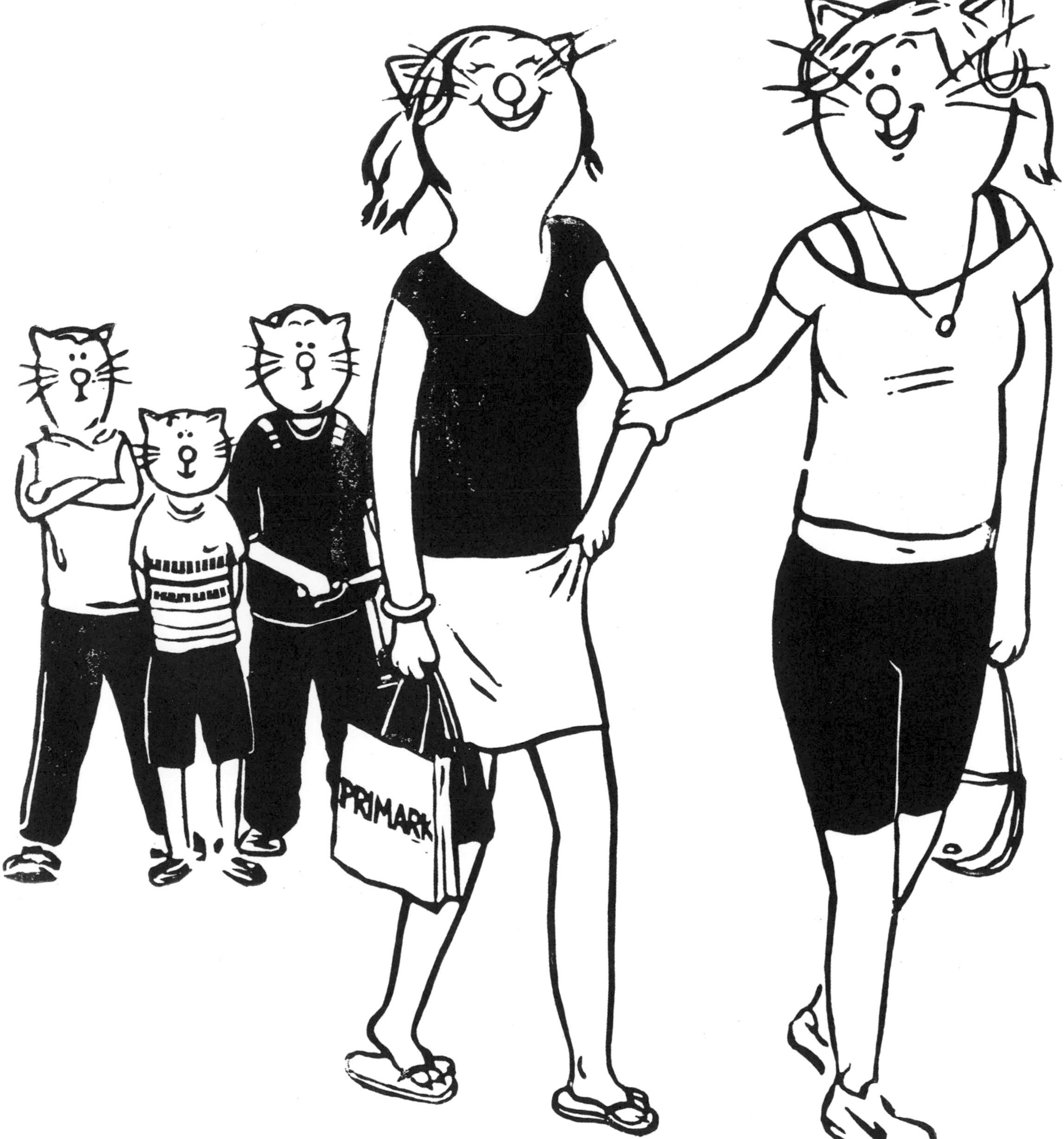
PRIMARK

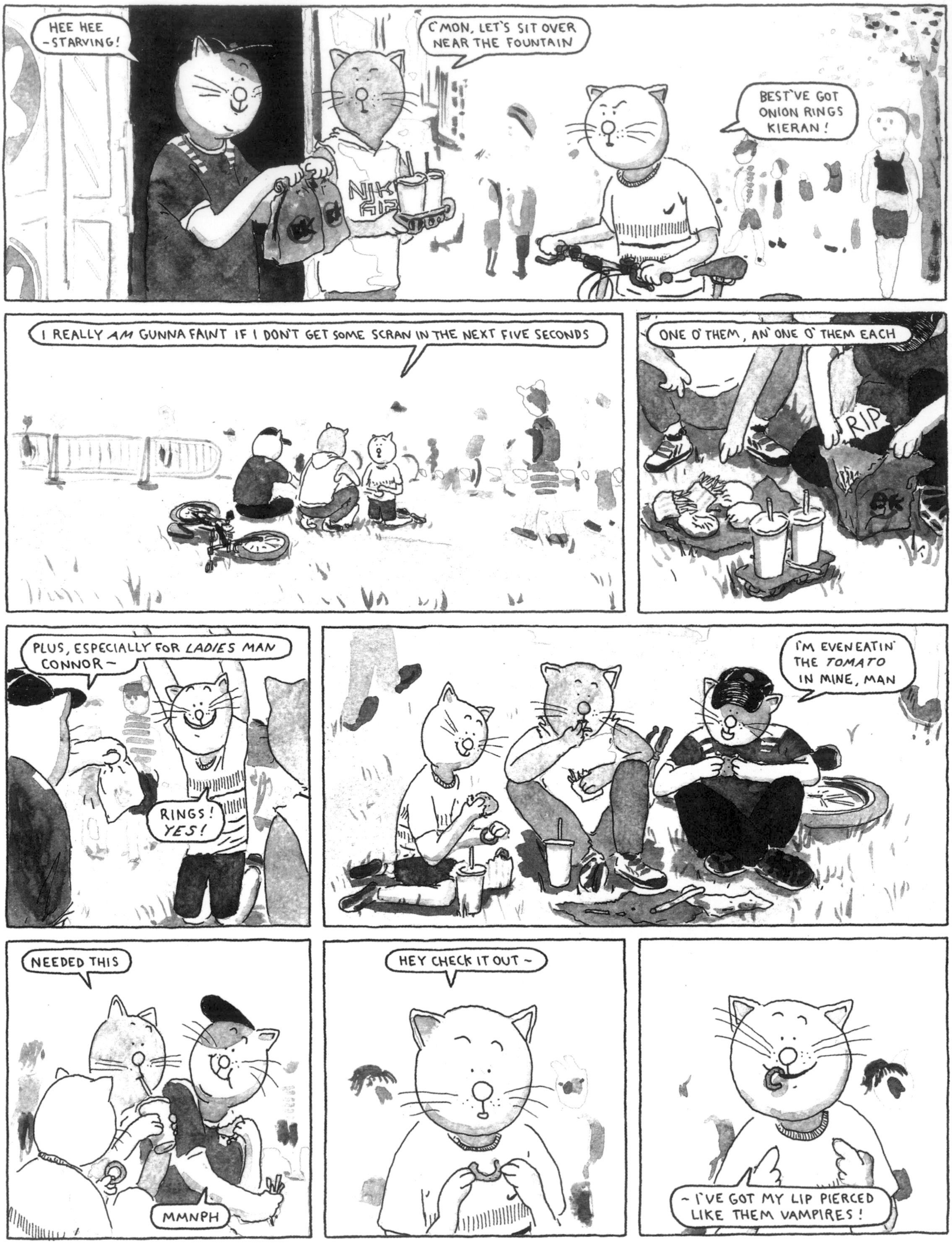
HEE HEE -STARVING!
C'MON, LET'S SIT OVER NEAR THE FOUNTAIN
BEST'VE GOT ONION RINGS KIERAN!
I REALLY AM GUNNA FAINT IF I DON'T GET SOME SCRAN IN THE NEXT FIVE SECONDS
ONE O' THEM, AN' ONE O' THEM EACH
RIP
PLUS, ESPECIALLY FOR LADIES MAN CONNOR~
RINGS! YES!
I'M EVEN EATIN' THE TOMATO IN MINE, MAN
NEEDED THIS
MMNPH
HEY CHECK IT OUT ~
~ I'VE GOT MY LIP PIERCED LIKE THEM VAMPIRES!

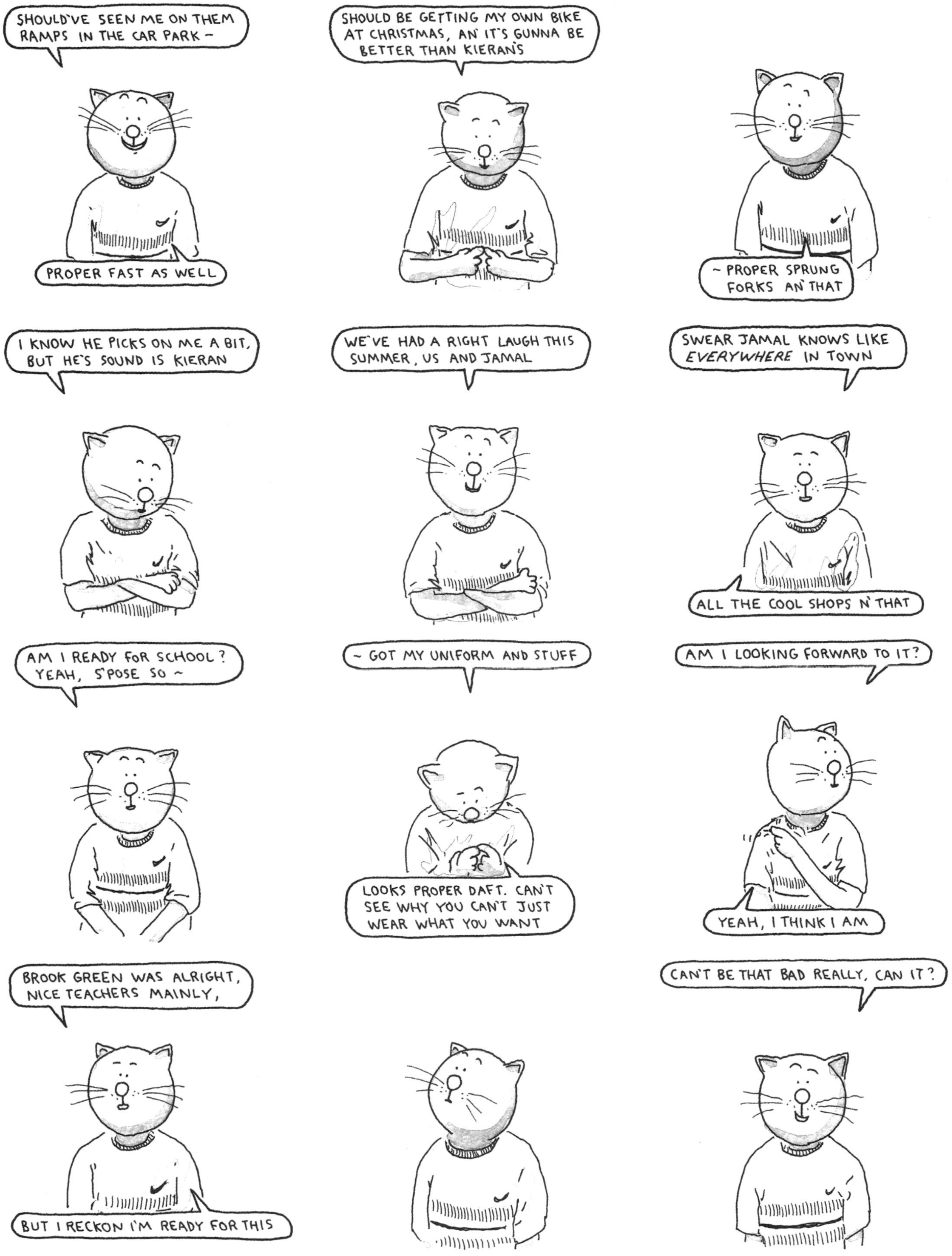

SHOULD'VE SEEN ME ON THEM RAMPS IN THE CAR PARK ~
PROPER FAST AS WELL
SHOULD BE GETTING MY OWN BIKE AT CHRISTMAS, AN' IT'S GUNNA BE BETTER THAN KIERAN'S
~ PROPER SPRUNG FORKS AN' THAT
I KNOW HE PICKS ON ME A BIT, BUT HE'S SOUND IS KIERAN
WE'VE HAD A RIGHT LAUGH THIS SUMMER, US AND JAMAL
SWEAR JAMAL KNOWS LIKE EVERYWHERE IN TOWN
ALL THE COOL SHOPS N' THAT
AM I READY FOR SCHOOL? YEAH, S'POSE SO ~
~ GOT MY UNIFORM AND STUFF
LOOKS PROPER DAFT. CAN'T SEE WHY YOU CAN'T JUST WEAR WHAT YOU WANT
AM I LOOKING FORWARD TO IT?
YEAH, I THINK I AM
BROOK GREEN WAS ALRIGHT, NICE TEACHERS MAINLY,
BUT I RECKON I'M READY FOR THIS
CAN'T BE THAT BAD REALLY, CAN IT?

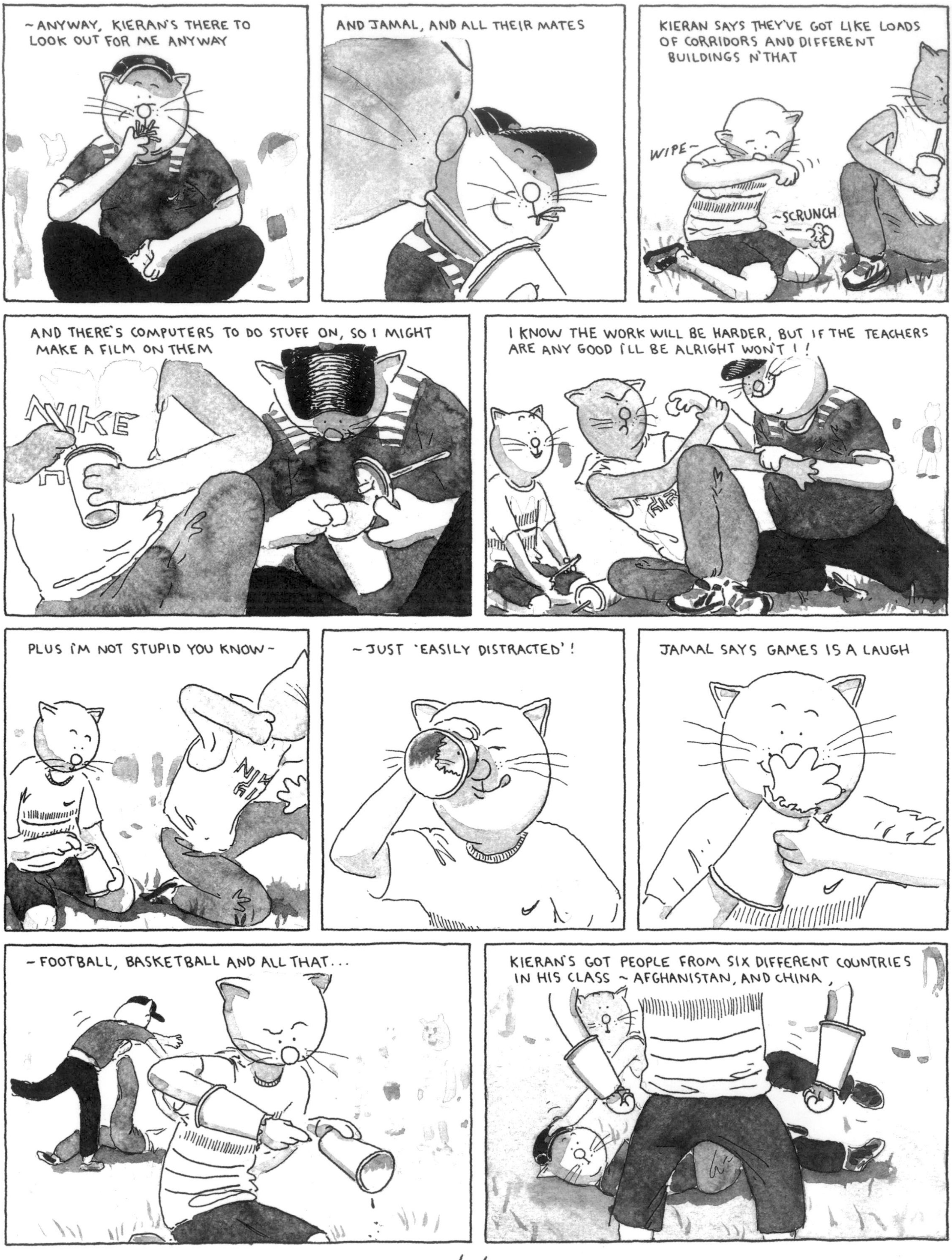
~ANYWAY, KIERAN'S THERE TO LOOK OUT FOR ME ANYWAY
AND JAMAL, AND ALL THEIR MATES
KIERAN SAYS THEY'VE GOT LIKE LOADS OF CORRIDORS AND DIFFERENT BUILDINGS N'THAT
WIPE~
~SCRUNCH
AND THERE'S COMPUTERS TO DO STUFF ON, SO I MIGHT MAKE A FILM ON THEM
NIKE
I KNOW THE WORK WILL BE HARDER, BUT IF THE TEACHERS ARE ANY GOOD I'LL BE ALRIGHT WON'T I!
PLUS I'M NOT STUPID YOU KNOW~
~JUST 'EASILY DISTRACTED'!
JAMAL SAYS GAMES IS A LAUGH
~FOOTBALL, BASKETBALL AND ALL THAT...
KIERAN'S GOT PEOPLE FROM SIX DIFFERENT COUNTRIES IN HIS CLASS ~ AFGHANISTAN, AND CHINA,

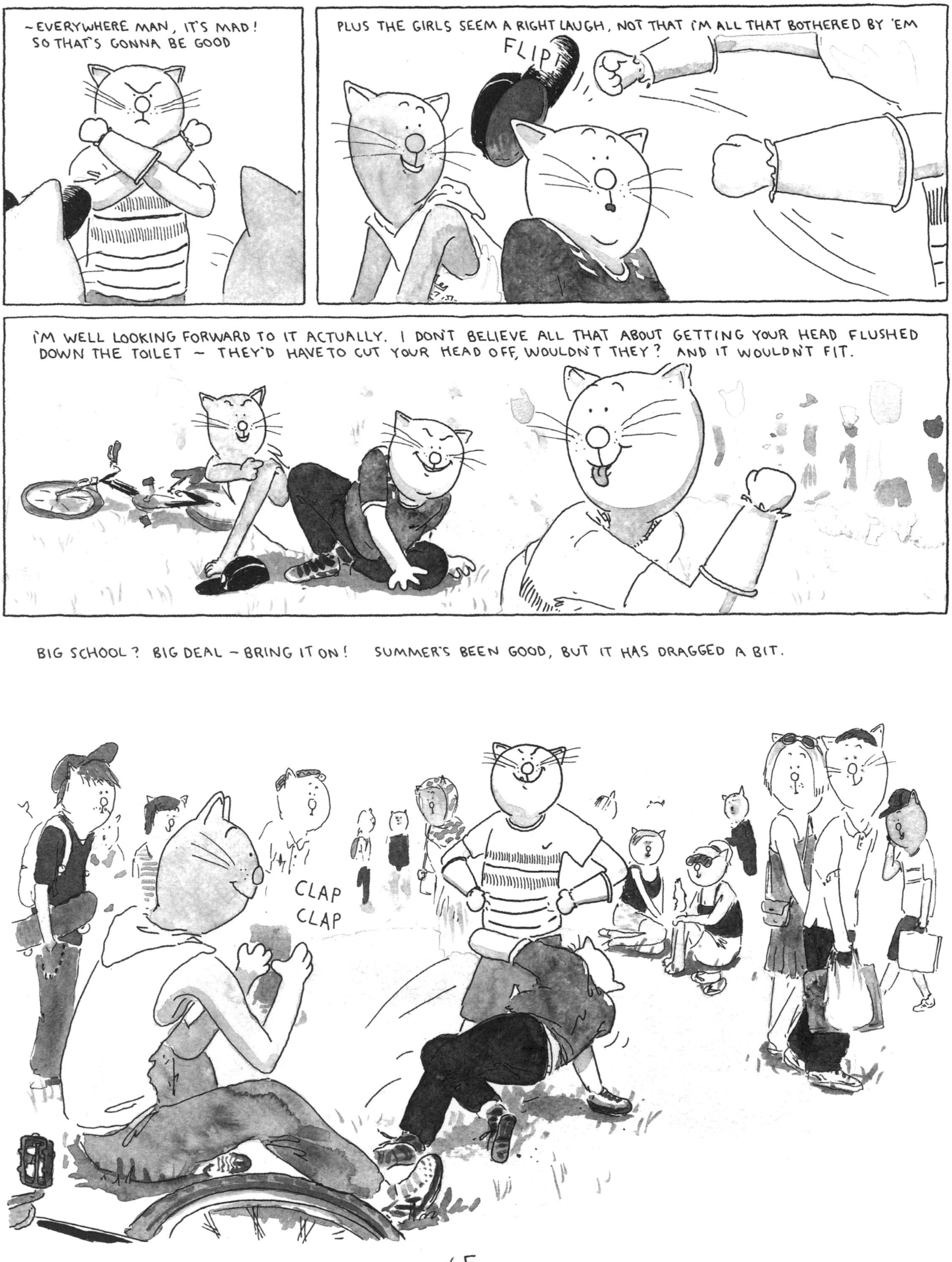
~EVERYWHERE MAN, IT'S MAD! SO THAT'S GONNA BE GOOD
PLUS THE GIRLS SEEM A RIGHT LAUGH, NOT THAT I'M ALL THAT BOTHERED BY 'EM
FLIP!
I'M WELL LOOKING FORWARD TO IT ACTUALLY. I DON'T BELIEVE ALL THAT ABOUT GETTING YOUR HEAD FLUSHED DOWN THE TOILET ~ THEY'D HAVE TO CUT YOUR HEAD OFF, WOULDN'T THEY? AND IT WOULDN'T FIT.
BIG SCHOOL? BIG DEAL ~ BRING IT ON!
SUMMER'S BEEN GOOD, BUT IT HAS DRAGGED A BIT.
CLAP
CLAP

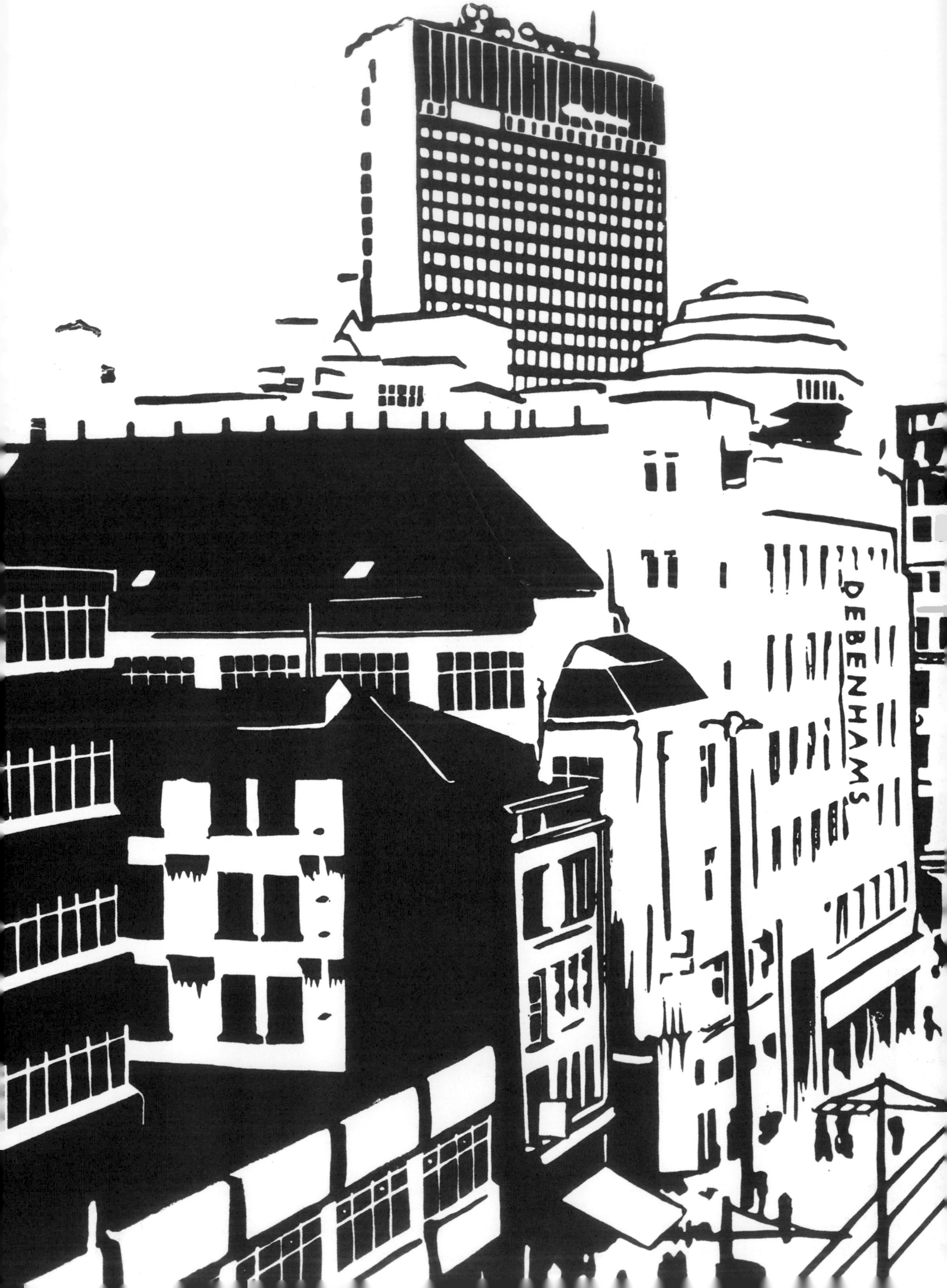
DEBENHAMS

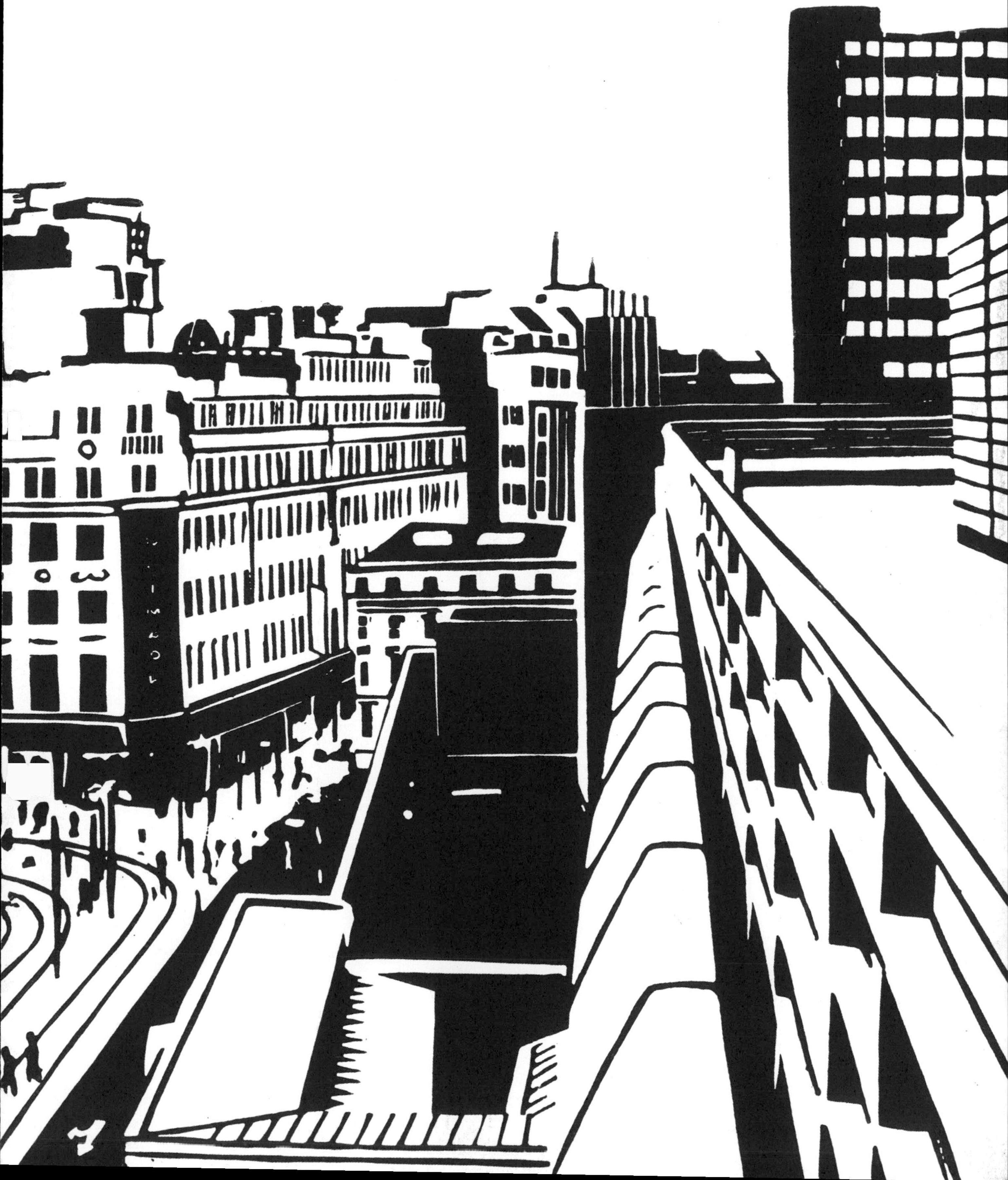

 This book is for Katy.

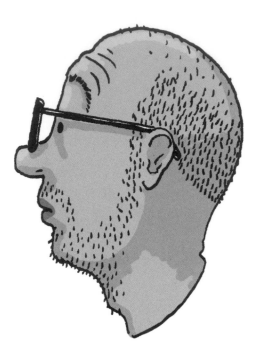

Playing Out © Jim Medway 2013
Slate 52

ISBN 978-1-906653-57-6

Chalk Marks is an imprint of Blank Slate Books
Publisher: Kenny Penman
Group Editor: Iz Rips
Art Director: Woodrow Phoenix
Publisher's assistant: Martin Steenton

The right of Jim Medway to be identified as the author of this work
has been asserted by him in accordance with the
Copyrights, Designs and Patents Act 1988.

Keep up with Jim at: http://pawqualitycomics.blogspot.co.uk

Discover more about Blank Slate:
online: www.blankslatebooks.co.uk
Facebook: blankslatebooks
twitter: @blankslatebooks

Jim has drawn the weekly strips **New at the Zoo** and
Crab Lane Crew for The DFC, and **Chip Charlton & Mr
Woofles of the Royal Canadian Mounted Police** for The
Phoenix. He has self-published **Teen Witch** and **Garden
Funnies,** and is hand-painting a new sign for Furness Vale
Fish Bar.
Since 2006 he has been running Create Comics workshops
for all ages across the country.

Thanks to Eddie.

Thanks to the Arts Council for their support.

All incidents and characters in Playing Out are fictional.